Holy Week

Proclamation 4

Aids for Interpreting
the Lessons of the Church Year

Holy Week

Richard I. Pervo

Series B

FORTRESS PRESS   **MINNEAPOLIS**

PROCLAMATION 4
Aids for Interpreting the Lessons of the Church Year
Series B: Holy Week

Scripture quotations unless otherwise noted are from the New Revised Standard Version of the Bible, copyright © 1989 by the Division of Christian Education of the National Council of the Churches of Christ in the United States of America.

Library of Congress Cataloging-in-Publication Data

(Revised for ser. B, vols. 1–4)

Proclamation 4.

   Consists of 24 volumes in 3 series designated A, B, and C, which correspond to the cycles of the three year lectionary. Each series contains 8 basic volumes with the following titles: [1] Advent-Christmas, [2] Epiphany, [3] Lent, [4] Holy Week, [5] Easter, [6] Pentecost 1, [7] Pentecost 2, and [8] Pentecost 3. In addition there are four volumes on the lesser festivals.
   By Christopher R. Seitz and others.
   Includes bibliographies.
   1. Bible—Homiletical use.   2. Bible—Liturgical lessons, English.   3. Bible—Criticism, interpretation, etc.   4. Common lectionary.   5. Church year.
I. Seitz, Christopher R.   II. Title: Proclamation four.
BS534.5.P765   1990   251   88-10982
ISBN 0-8006-4172-8 (series B, Holy Week)

The paper used in this publication meets the minimum requirements of American National Standard for Information Sciences—Permanence of Paper for Printed Library Materials, ANSI Z329.48-1984.   ∞™

Manufactured in the U.S.A.   AF 1-4172
94   93   92   91   90   1   2   3   4   5   6   7   8   9   10

Contents

Introduction

What is the purpose of the observance of the church year and to what do we owe its origins? The earliest Christian annual festival was the *Pascha,* a single celebration of the death and resurrection of Christ, coordinated with the Jewish observance of Passover. Our present Holy Week (of eight days) results from the vivid impact upon pilgrims of the practices in late fourth-century Jerusalem, where separate celebrations of various Gospel narratives took place at their traditional sites. Success bred imitation, bringing with it a potential for historicizing the gospel and for separating the event of redemption into discrete components.

Yet another layer emerges with the concept of the *triduum sacrum,* the three most holy days, once Friday through Sunday, then later beginning on Thursday evening before Easter. The liturgies of Maundy Thursday, Good Friday, and the Great Vigil constitute the definitive core of the church year and set forth the nature and meaning of Christian existence. Holy Week, as a unified liturgical progression or historical reenactment, therefore does not really exist. Palm/Passion Sunday has as a prelude a rehearsal of Jesus' entry, but the liturgy proper has as its focus the Passion, the subject once more on Good Friday. The pastoral problem of the varying patterns of attendance, with the largest attendance on Palm Sunday and Easter Morning, emerges because many miss the three principal liturgies of Maundy Thursday, Good Friday, and the Great Vigil.

What are preachers, burdened by the emotional and physical drain of this climactic week, to do? We may profit from some brief reflection upon the meaning of the Christian year. It is more than a psychologically sound educational scheme ascertaining that the faithful ponder in course the mysteries of salvation. It is also more than a means of determining that the diversity of Scripture receives its due. Every celebration seeks not only edification but also, and more importantly, *participation,* and is thus a sacramental proclamation of the entire gospel. The origins of this week in the single observance of *Pascha* provide a historical warrant for the preservation of its theological unity. One task of the proclaimer, then, is to keep the totality of redemption in view, to prevent the isolation of each observance.

In the face of this challenge stand the character, length, and frequency of services during Holy Week. The week does not call for one long sermon following another. Planning is highly desirable. Which theme, scene, symbol, or idea can one lift up from the welter of material as a means for the illustration and comprehension of the whole? How is the designated preacher to enhance, interpret, and apply the message, rather than offer an anticlimax or even an obstacle to it? Certainly this cannot happen apart from careful, general, and prayerful preparation.

The Scripture citations in this volume have been taken from the New Revised Standard Version (NRSV).

Sunday of the Passion
Palm Sunday

Lutheran	Roman Catholic	Episcopal	Common Lectionary
Zech. 9:9-10	Isa. 50:4-7	Isa. 45:21-25	Isa. 50:4-9a
Phil. 2:5-11	Phil. 2:6-11	Phil. 2:5-11	Phil. 2:5-11
Mark 14:1—15:47	Mark 14:1—15:47	Mark 14:1—15:47 or Mark 15:1-39	Mark 14:1—15:47 or Mark 15:1-39

The liturgical title gives priority to the Passion, for the liturgy of the palms is only an elaborate entrance rite providing a contrast to what follows.

FIRST LESSON

Lutheran: Zechariah 9:9-10. This reading serves as a bridge between the liturgy of the palms and the Passion narrative. It comes from the collection of oracles concluding the Minor Prophets and does not belong to the writing that constitutes Zechariah 1–8. By presenting the entrance of a humble king the passage provides comparison to and contrast with the second lesson from Philippians 2. The context utilizes the "divine warrior" metaphor for God, an image not popular in our age. On this Sunday, at least, it has the merit of stressing that the subject of the phrase "power in weakness" does not claim that lack of power is a virtue, but that weakness gives opportunity to accept dependence upon God. Like Jesus, this king receives support from one whose power does not meet ordinary standards and is thus unseen. The love of God, which is manifest in weakness, is far from powerless. The nameless king here portrayed is humble because his vindication has been wrought by God. He is thus comparable to the servant of Deutero-Isaiah.

His transport of choice is an ass. Although this animal belongs to the tradition, by the time of Jesus (if not long before) it would be incongruous, most unregal and unmilitary, like a president-elect going to the inauguration upon a bicycle. To early Christians the entry of a monarch was a familiar image of triumph and promise. The arrival (Greek *parousia*, Latin *adventus*) of a ruler in the capital was an event fraught with utopian and religious expectations and symbols. Jesus' entry is both an ironic parousia and a

9

foreshadowing of his appearance in the full power of the resurrection. Holy Week maintains the tension of both aspects of the entry. There is another blade with a double edge: Those who acclaim the entry of the great king waving their palms in procession will soon call for his crucifixion.

The Servant Songs. Because the Servant Songs of Deutero-Isaiah are a vital element of the readings for Holy Week, proclaimers might well read and study these as a whole rather than encounter them singly. Their author was an anonymous prophet active in Babylon during the latter period of the exile (587–539 BCE). Like the pre-exilic prophets he experienced a divine call. The central event of this age was the collapse of the apparently invincible evil empire, Babylon the Great, vanquisher of Judah and ravisher of the Temple. The prophet saw in this fall evidence for the supremacy of God and for divine rule over all nations, with the consequence that God was not bound to any political entity.

The Servant Songs are profoundly clear yet elusive poems. They seem to report aspects of a particular biography, but their subject remains anonymous. Is the servant the author, a figure of the future, a type, a collective representation, or all or none of these? In the mystery and elusiveness of the Servant Songs there lies one of the keys with which to unlock some of the mysteries of Holy Week. Tidy resolutions of poetic elusiveness may leave one contemplating a bit of banal prose.

Rather than approach these texts with apologetic glee or enlightened disdain, proclaimers will do well to learn from them that sometimes poetry is more revealing than history. The Servant Songs are also foundational texts, among the oracles most plumbed by early Christians seeking to find the meaning of their experience in reflection upon Scripture. That is a capacity far from exhausted. Jesus, who summons all to serve one another, will not be distraught if the descriptions fit many servants of God in addition to himself.

Roman Catholic/Common: Isaiah 50:4-9a. The formal model for this song is the psalm of individual lament, a type much utilized for explication of the Gospel accounts of Jesus' betrayal. Recognition of the underlying model leads to perception of how the prophet has transformed it.

Verses 4-5a employ the language of education. The prophet has been formed in a rough school, with God as the teacher and suffering as the curriculum. Earlier prophets, notably Jeremiah, did not consider their afflictions justified. The servant accepts them. His affirmation of God's presence and support is thus paradoxical. In the very depths of an affliction that cannot be dismissed as unmerited he exults in God's allegiance (vv. 6-9). The confession of power in weakness comes to light. The servant does not, despite the initial images of the schoolroom, suggest that suffering is of value because it is a useful learning exercise. Suffering has meaning because God is present with those who suffer and can sustain them in it.

With this confidence the servant can assert that his opponents only appear invincible and triumphant. They look good, like new clothes, but they are destined for eventual discard. Because the same images recur in the Passion, they provide an interpretive framework for it. The story of Jesus' sufferings is not told to elicit sympathy or to promote guilt but to present a model for behavior and a means for understanding. This Servant Song illuminates the cross because it speaks of victory, not of defeat quickly relieved by a miracle, nor of tragedy producing ennervating remorse.

The legal language that permeates vv. 8-9a sheds hermeneutical light upon the trial of Jesus. Verdicts of heavenly and earthly courts do not always coincide. To claim legal vindication in the face of juridical execution is to confess utter confidence in the judgment of God. This song speaks not only to the situation of Jesus but to all who find themselves in societies obsessed with personal satisfaction and the signs of success. The prophet, who is anything but indifferent to world affairs and is no political quietist, raises the questions of real versus apparent victory and whether seeming triumph is the mark of God's approval.

For Christians the Passion of Jesus is the ultimate answer to these questions. This lesson is not so much background to the Passion as comment upon it, comment that supplies us with appreciation for both the continuity of revelation through history and its discontinuity with human values.

Episcopal: Isaiah 45:21-25. (Those who choose to read Genesis 22 or Wisdom 2 on Good Friday will presumably assign Isaiah 52–53 to this occasion.)

Verse 23 contains an obvious link to Phil. 2:10, which cites it. More important are its form—a trial speech—and its cosmic scope. To make these factors clear, the lector should begin with v. 20a, then proceed to v. 21 (20b is probably a gloss). The defendants called into God's dock are the once-proud vanquishers of Jerusalem, the now crushed Babylonians. At this moment of victory God does not gloat or indulge in "I told you so's". There is instead an offer of salvation, an extension to these pagans of the benefits resident in election as chosen people. Their defeat is an opportunity to acknowledge that God is indeed God. The vicissitudes of history judge all claims of human authorities to be eternal and infallible sovereigns of world destiny. So the judge sentences the guilty to a sentence of deliverance.

This God's ways are not our ways. Another illustration of this principle is the cross. The cross also speaks to the vanquished. It is an ensign of defeat summoning those without hope to find in it victory. God rules the world but eschews the methods of imperialism, inviting rather than coercing. God is judge of all but permits the world to formulate its own future.

By acclaiming the universal sweep of salvation this text summons Christians to look beyond themselves during Holy Week, to recognize that hope does not come from ignoring historical events and the realities of daily life. Whom shall we regard as the defeated here addressed? Ourselves alone, or the wretched of the earth as well? Many early Christians saw themselves as beleaguered and oppressed by Jews. That situation no longer applies. Holy Week is no time for denunciation, at least not by those who hear the message of Isaiah 45:21-25, and accept it.

SECOND LESSON: PHILIPPIANS 2:5-11

Verse 5 is essential to this passage, for it contains the ethical imperative arising from the creedal indicative of the following verses. Early Christian exhortations usually begin with statements of salvation (indicative) that constitute the how and why of the subsequent directions for living (imperative). Why does Philippians invert the scheme, and why does the indicative take the form of a hymn?

There is general agreement that vv. 6-11 are an early Christian hymn of pre-Pauline origin, although its structure is debated. Like John 1:1-18 it proceeds from the identification of Christ with heavenly wisdom, but it also apparently makes use of speculation about the primal Adam and—of great significance in the liturgical setting—it appears to have been shaped by the kind of interpretation of the Servant Songs found in The Wisdom of Solomon 2–5. The cohesion is not fortuitous and reveals that early Christians explored the Songs to find theological rather than merely historical insights.

What does it mean to present theology in the form of poetry? Both must work with the language of metaphor and symbol, as Thomas Aquinas noted. Like the hymns associated with the veneration of the cross on Good Friday, this passage explains the meaning of the crucifixion and extols its victory. It is a comment upon the Passion in advance, a few lofty and carefully crafted phrases that prepare one for what is to follow without spoiling the story. There is much here from which preachers can learn.

Paul probably added "even death on a cross" to the familiar text. That act served as both the basest moment of humiliation and the very impetus for divine action. The crucifixion set God loose, as it were. Philippians 2 contains no reference to resurrection, preventing any approach that sees the cross as an apparent disaster followed by speedy deliverance. The victory of the cross here resonates in all its paradoxical power and perfection. The might of God came into play when by all reasonable views Jesus had been crushed by vastly superior forces. The one exalted and given obeisance by all is the one crucified.

Equality with God was not "something to be exploited." These words shatter the fabric of a universe bent upon exploiting all of the power and status attainable. Paul's admonition is not an invitation to a kind of moralistic humility, a quality both irritating and often exploited to control others. Community life, not individual demeanor, is the subject under consideration. Paul argues that the community is bound together with the "mind" of Christ Jesus, with his example and with his essence. This is perhaps the most vital, not to say crucial, aspect of the passage for Passion Sunday, which seeks to incorporate all within the life of Christ through participation in his experience.

Such incorporation into such a life runs vastly counter to the contemporary impetuses toward viewing self-fulfillment and self-realization as the hallmark of human vocation. At this juncture the scandal of the cross becomes manifest. To bow before the raised cross is to renounce the dominant notions about what life means and should be. The mind of Christ promotes equality as freedom to serve others, not as power to exploit in self-service. This is, of course, a view presented in narrative form by the evangelist known to us as Mark.

GOSPEL: MARK 14:1—15:47

The Passion according to Mark. It is pastorally desirable that the entire Passion be proclaimed, read or sung, with participation by all, and with more regard for solemnity than for gimmickry. The setting and text present a considerable challenge to preachers. There are many options, including selection of a theme relevant to the situation of the community, the pursuit and explication of a particular recurrent image, or narrowing upon a particular section or episode to serve as a homiletic synecdoche. The following general exposition intends to provide stimulus and resources for various strategies. Similarities to and contrasts with the Johannine Passion suggest the benefits of reading the commentaries upon both prior to Passion Sunday. Year B is scripturally rich in that Mark and John view the Passion from a kindred theological perspective yet express it in quite different ways. The opportunity to hear each within five days allows worshipers to see beyond the outward frame of each evangelist to truths beyond words. The most obvious contrast lies in Mark's depiction of a very human and suffering Jesus, with whom each may fully identify, and John's majestic protagonist, who offers us the assurance of a divine savior unvanquished by the world he has come to redeem.

St. Mark's Passion slashes us with its relentless exposure of our Lord's stark and tragic humanity. Few tales appear to speak so poignantly yet with such artless simplicity. This latter impression is quite deceptive, for here, at the heart and climax of the Gospel, the evangelist has not stepped back to let unedited sources speak for themselves. All of the major themes of Mark culminate in 14:1—16:8. The genre behind the gospel stories of Jesus' Passion is the tale of the suffering righteous person, a type developed in the wisdom tradition for expression of its ideal but adaptable for a variety of theological expressions. The clarity of its structure contributes to that deceptive impression of artlessness. The tradition of Gospel harmonization encourages concentration upon individual episodes, but the meaning of this material emerges from their arrangement. Some of the more important literary techniques include the division of one unit or episode to frame another and a fondness for groups of three.

Whereas the first ten chapters of Mark march with almost breathless swiftness, the action begins to slow from the moment Jesus reaches Jerusalem. The author devotes fifteen percent of his text to the twenty-four hours beginning on Thursday evening. Chapter 14 introduces a major narrative shift. The authorities' efforts at leading Jesus into reckless speech have failed; they now begin to plot treachery (14:1-2). Only one factor counsels delay: the need to work behind the backs of the holiday throngs. Passover is nearly at hand. That it is the celebration of deliverance from tyranny bothers the leaders not at all. For the readers "Passover" is an ironic and ominous word. The popularity of Jesus with the masses remains unabated. Between this notice of their plans and the opportune arrival of Judas Mark "sandwiches" the story of the anointing.

14:1-12: Misunderstanding, Rejection, and Betrayal.   As chapter 14 opens Jesus has a number of followers who do not understand him but remain. At its close he has none. Two have primary roles: Judas and Peter. Although the former is bent upon betrayal and the latter upon confession, they come to similar ends. All of the scenes discuss discipleship in contrast to betrayal. The verb *betray* is a *leitmotif,* occurring some ten times in the

Passion. God's plan continues to unfold, despite human shortcomings. The fear of the disciples is theological, not psychological. The foreknowledge they are granted only enhances the depth of their final failure.

(For discussion of *14:3-9* see the entry for Monday, where it is the alternate Episcopal Gospel. For discussion of *14:12-26* see Holy Thursday, where it is the Lutheran Gospel.)

14:26-52: Departure, Gethsemane, and Arrest. Like the account of the supper, this material includes three scenes. The theme is endurance, illustrated by its absence.

Jesus' prediction of his disciples' flight constitutes a parallel to vv. 18-21. The scriptural citation shows that this is in accordance with prophecy and thus part of the divine plan. Verse 28 looks to an eventual reversal, providing further reassurance for the reader and no comment from the disciples. Peter will not be put to flight by Bible verses. Two cockcrows bespeak momentous blindness. Mark 13:35 provides this exchange with a broader application. Peter and the others will not be awake, for they will seek to preserve their skins (cf. 15:29-32 and 8:35). Peter's failure symbolizes theological misunderstanding. His "must" (v. 31) is like a parody of the Passion predictions (8:31, etc.). The rest chime unwittingly in, just as "they all drank" of the cup (14:23).

Mark has shaped the Gethsemane account (vv. 32-42) from traditions (cf. Heb. 5:7, John 12:27f.). This is not a sentimental story. Here and in the following scene discipleship unravels, reversing (as it were) 1:14-20, kerygma and call. This connection between these two scenes is signalled by the repetition in 14:42 of the precise verb-form used in 1:15 (*ēngiken*) and the selection of Peter, James, and John—three of the first four disciples from Mark 1. The tradition of the Maundy Thursday watch is one expression of the paradigmatic character of this passage, which speaks to the church during the time of Jesus' absence. Mark has prepared the reader by the account of discipleship in 10:35-40 and the parabolic conclusion to Jesus' address in 13:33-37. Both passages have verbal echoes in vv. 32-42. The vividness and density of these allusions are aspects of the careful crafting of this crucial unit.

There are three subscenes. Jesus radiates his full and unrestrained humanness. His prayers are models for the church. The disciples' sleep is a spiritual and theological condition. They are dull to the meaning of Jesus' "hour," and fall prey to temptation while he is absent. Jesus' deepest union with God occurs here, not at the baptism and transfiguration, not amidst signs of a wondrous epiphany, but in anticipation of his coming death.

Verses 41-42 bring together the hour (13:32), the betrayal, and the arrest. The difficult verb rendered "enough" in v. 41 is an accounting term. The bill for the cost of discipleship is being presented after the meal. Jesus steels himself to meet his betrayer, who does not take him unawares.

The arresting party includes representatives of the groups who have opposed Jesus in Jerusalem, together with a crowd, waving swords and clubs now, not branches. They are depicted like a mob. The kiss is a traditional feature (Prov. 27:6; 2 Sam. 15:5; 20:8-10) underlying the monstrosity of betrayal by the closest of intimates. Whom does the "bystander" who does violence represent? Let those who have ears hear. These do not. Jesus' saying exposes the tactics of his attackers. Authorities like to call their opponents "terrorists." Mark 11:15-17 suggests that the true terrorists are those managing the Temple. Jesus sets his integrity over and against the chicanery of his arresters. The reference to Scripture in v. 49 serves as a reminder of who is really in charge. The climax comes quickly and devastatingly in v. 50: Those whom he has called leave him and flee.

Does the brief and enigmatic episode of the youth (vv. 51-52) reinforce this by showing one who gave up all, even his clothing, to abandon Jesus? Does his self-stripping and humiliation made in a desperate attempt to secure his own life contrast with the fate of Jesus? Or does his nudity represent the state of those who once occupied another garden—as well as the state of those being baptized? Jesus, covered with a linen cloth, fled death at the resurrection, leaving the sheet behind. The youth may symbolize those who die and rise with Christ in baptism, having put off their old clothing and nature, accepting with their Lord the nakedness of exposure and "death" by water, entombment in the font and emergence to new life. Those who visit Jesus' tomb will encounter a young person also, likewise dressed in white, to proclaim the message (14:51-52; 15:46; 16:5). All of the mystery of the Passion resides within these two brief verses. The question of triumph or tragedy is difficult to resolve. The ambiguity is not accidental and will not go away, not here, not at the cross, nor even at the tomb.

14:53—15:15: Trials and Judgment.   Mark relates a trial by the Sanhedrin in 14:53—15:1, and another before Pilate in 15:2-15b. Each contains an inserted subplot that will provide contrast and interpretation. Peter, who represents the believers, denies his Lord while Jesus holds fast to his confession. The heretofore friendly crowd definitively rejects Jesus. They wish a messiah who is a winner. Peter replays his earlier reluctance to follow a messiah who is bound for the cross (8:32-33). The trials follow a parallel format. God and Caesar converge because the priestly leaders would render the same (in this case Jesus) to each.

14:54, 66-72: Peter's Denial. This is a simple and powerful tragedy performed by quite humble characters, a Galilean, a slave, and some bystanders. There are three subscenes, each increasing in fervor and enlarging in audience. Links with other material are abundant. Bystanders were present at the arrest and will be present at the cross. Mark 4:16-17 spoke of what happens to seed falling upon rocky (Peter!) soil: In trouble or persecution it falls away. "You are" (v. 70) echoes Peter's confession (8:29). To be "with Jesus" (v. 67) means discipleship (3:14, 5:18). Peter's "I do not know" contrasts with the demons who say "I know who you are" (e.g., 1:24). "Outside" (v. 68) refers to nonfollowers (e.g., 4:11). "Truly" occurs only once elsewhere, in the acclamation of the centurion (15:39). Only Herod also swears an oath (6:23), thus linking the deaths of Jesus and John the Baptizer. The scene is thus thick with allusions to the rest of the Gospel and works as a climactic summary of its message about discipleship.

At utter variance with the above is the behavior of Jesus who in response to the question makes the confession that leads to his death. Mark blends trial and denial into simultaneous stories. The ambiguity of Peter's curse is deliberate, for to curse Jesus is to curse one's self (8:38). Those who would confess Jesus as the Christ must follow and be with him. Anything else is curse, not confession.

Proclamation of Gethsemane and Peter's denial ought not dip into platitudes ("even mighty Peter stumbled"), slip into sentiment ("see how he weeps"), invoke psychology ("the poor disciples were exhausted by stress"), or engage in polemic ("How dumb can you be?"). Gethsemane presents a lesson on discipleship as vigilance. Peter's denial is a narrative explanation of the baptismal creed.

The Sanhedrin trial opens with a foray of futile efforts to convict Jesus with crooked testimony. The statement about the new Temple looks like unwitting prophecy, but the notion may not be congenial to Mark. After this tactic has for the last time (cf. chaps. 11–12) collapsed of its own weight, the high priest takes matters into his own hands and tries a new ploy: direct interrogation. Jesus does not disappoint them. The high priest's question is framed in creedal fashion, verbally identical to Peter's statement at 8:29 (irony upon irony!). This applies to the reader. Only in this context, when misinterpretation can be excluded does Jesus say "yes," but, as in 8:30, he immediately interprets his kingship by reference to the Son of man (cf. 13:26 and, on "you will see," 16:7). This is a packed statement, the result of much theological activity, bringing together Ps. 110:1 and Dan. 7:13. What epiphany will the high priests witness? That of 15:31? For Mark, "Son of Man" refers to a messiah who suffers as servant of all, to a messiah who confounds all expectations. It is not material to provide rationalizations for how the Sanhedrin discovered blasphemy. They may be left to their own rationalizations, the basis of which is the possession of an avowed pretender whom they can deliver to Caesar's agent. That is where he will be sent, but first they take the opportunity to vent their frustrations with some personal abuse, before giving him to the guards for a serious beating. All of this is mere official brutality, not punishment, for the sentence is yet to come. Their demand that Jesus prophesy has its irony, for he has fulfilled the role of the prophet rejected by his own people.

Pilate raises the same points with questions shaped by Christian experiences and needs. The trial accounts would serve others called before the rulers of society. In this instance Jesus' reply is more equivocal. To be sure Pilate would have no chance of grasping a statement about the Son of man, but this response emphasizes the ambiguity of Jesus' kingship. Does he say "in your terms, yes," meaning that he is indeed a threat to Caesar's order, or simply shift the burden to Pilate?

Mark 15:6-15 portrays the choice between Jesus and Barabbas (a would-be "son of the father"), and introduces the crowd, who, like Peter, "deny" Jesus. However, in their case they do so because they elect the avenue of political revolt (a discredited option by the time Mark appeared). They affirm their choice three times, as have others. Jesus has brought life. The crowd prefers one with hands stained by blood. Pilate here plays the role of Herod (6:14-29) and the mob that of Herodias' daughter. Jesus and John meet similar fates.

The mockery following Pilate's judgment sets out in ironic narrative form the meaning of power in weakness. The secular powers unwittingly attest to a reality that their self-interest prevents them from comprehending. Jesus is king in a servile state, having humbled himself. The leader is slave of all. This is a mock epiphany of a divine ruler, hailed by the adoring throngs of his soldiery while clad in imperial purple and wearing the radiant crown of deity. This conclusion intends to show, in a highly realistic fashion, that the Pilate trial is a microcosm of the difference between political appearances and social realities. When this entertainment has run its course, Jesus is stripped for humiliation, then reclothed, having put off the form of the divine ruler to assume the likeness of a servant.

15:16-47: Crucifixion, Death, and Burial. One should regard with suspicion descriptions of crucifixion that know and elaborate each fixed detail and even venture to provide medical opinions. The procedure was not fixed by rubrics, nor do manuals about it survive. Allowance was made for local conditions, particular circumstances, and the all-too-rich resources of sadistic invention. We do not know, for example, whether drugged wine would have been offered as an act of kindness or as a refinement of cruelty intended to prolong the ordeal.

Mark does not focus upon the details of Jesus' suffering, nor does he seek to arouse pathos through sensational detail. For a contrast see 4 Maccabees. To recount these events early Christians made frequent and thoughtful recourse to Scripture, in which God's will was revealed.

The way of the cross (vv. 20b-22) makes a reverse of the entry recalled earlier this day. Jesus entered in a kind of regal procession; he leaves in a Roman procession. At the entry crowds came from the fields; now comes a single representative, impressed from the field (11:18; 15:21). The need to draft Simon points to the failure of the Twelve and portrays what disciples should do.

Verses 22-27. Jesus is stripped prior to being baptized into death (cf. 10:38f.). The title is the second Roman inscription to appear (12:13-17). Both evoke sarcasm and irony. Also ironic upon more than one level is the accompaniment of two insurrectionists. On the one hand they show the official view of Jesus; on another they take the places on left and right sought earlier by James and John, who are unavailable (10:35-40).

Verses 27-32: Mockery. There are three groups, each associated with a scriptural citation. The bystanders represent the people whose religion and patriotism center upon the Temple. For the high priests the title "christ" is a threat to their existence. In the absence of disciples, the bandits curse and revile Jesus, as had Peter. The mockery is christological. Miracle-mongers demand proof, seeing before believing (cf. John 20:29). If Jesus is the kind of messiah they require, there will be a last-minute rescue. Some contemporary popular novels did depict heroes delivered from the cross. Mark mocks such romance. To see Jesus one must gaze upon the one dying upon the cross and believe in him. Any Christology that rejects the cross is built upon sinking sand. Salvation comes from surrender of one's self into the hands of God (8:34, of believers; 10:45, of the redeemer).

Verses 33-39: Death. This passage parallels the epiphanies at Jesus' baptism and transfiguration (1:9-11; 9:2-8). Each includes cosmic signs, a voice, and an acclamation. In the death scene darkness falls (the time of Passover), the temple curtain splits (1:10 and 15:38 use the same verb), Jesus emits a loud "voice" (literally), and the acclamation comes from a Roman officer. Darkness is symbolic of chaos in the cosmic sphere, and the curtain of chaos in the religiopolitical realm, for the cult was believed to sustain the fabric of the universe. Another apocalyptic symbol is the time frame (15:25, 33, 34a), revealing God's hand behind all (compare the enumeration of the days of creation). Darkness is a phenomenon of catastrophe, the day of the Lord, and death. The "loud cry" is in Mark linked to the destruction of evil, and is thus a feature of exorcisms. Through this symbolic apparatus the evangelist portrays the crucifixion as the climactic struggle with, and victory over, evil. The powers appear supreme. In reality they have been vanquished, because the death of Jesus is the saving act of God. The Temple has no more function. One can't mend an old garment with a new patch (2:21-28).

Jesus dies as the very human "Son of man." Ambiguity rules, even amidst signs. The loud shout could be no more than a scream of pain or the protest of an innocent. In Mark, Jesus' cry of dereliction is the only "word of Jesus from the cross," expressing with stark humanity the anguish of one deserted by all, yet able to say "*my* God." For the onlookers this presents one more chance to mock by imagining that Elijah is being summoned. Some fantasize theologies of glory even in the face of the cross. Revelation remains always uncertain so that it may invite rather than compel.

At the supreme moment the acclamation of Jesus as Son of God comes not from a celestial voice but from a gentile soldier. What he saw, and even what he said, remain mysterious. He does not convert and leave his post. Mark's readers, mostly Gentiles, are invited to share this confession and upon no more evidence than assurance of Jesus' death as a selfless surrender of life. The only other witnesses noted are those women who, since 14:3, have been the only faithful disciples. Three are named, in counterpoint to Peter, James, and John, as those who serve and, albeit at some distance, become the bearers of the tradition.

Verses 42-47: Burial.   For the accounts of Jesus' burial early Christians were prepared to let legend flourish, for this is a narrative form of the creedal formula: "Jesus died, and was buried" (cf. 1 Cor. 15:3-5). Such details as the secure tomb, postmortem veneration by a wealthy and pious gentleman, and a resting place refuting any suggestion that the deceased was a criminal, serve to proclaim Jesus' death as a victory and thus constitute a proper interpretive conclusion to the Passion.

Welcome as such vindication might be, it is little enough. The burial is also ambiguous. Has the story come to an end with death as the enemy's last word? The onset of the Sabbath suggests that the story is beginning once more (cf. 1:20-34). This introduces suspense, and a note of hope.

The Passion is no neat package. We cannot wrap it up, for it seeks to envelop us all. Traditional practice omits the acclamation customary at the conclusion of the Gospel. The only meaningful response is with our lives, and thus we relive this action each year to gain courage so that we may not flee but take up our cross and follow Jesus to victory.

Monday in Holy Week

Lutheran	Roman Catholic	Episcopal	Common Lectionary
Isa. 42:1-9	Isa. 42:1-7	Isa. 42:1-9	Isa. 42:1-9
Heb. 9:11-15		Heb.11:39—12:3	Heb. 9:11-15
John 12:1-11	John 12:1-11	John 12:1-11 *or* Mark 14:3-9	John 12:1-11

FIRST LESSON: ISAIAH 42:1-7(9)

This is a famous passage, evocative yet mixed. The oracle proper runs through v. 4, with vv. 5-9 as an interpretive expansion. "Justice" is the refrain of the opening section while universality is the theme of the second part. Some of the images suggest a king, others a prophet. Like Moses, God's servant, this one is both leader and inspired religious figure. His leadership will not follow the normal course of public display, and the judgment he brings will not conform to the kind of realism that orders dim wicks quenched and broken reeds pruned away. The justice he is called to establish will not have the traditional chauvinistic focus. Through him the nations are to experience deliverance and illumination.

The motive for this mission lies in the character of a God who has formed the universe and fashioned every human being, yet, like a caring mother, can take the servant by the hand and lead him to open blind eyes and shatter prison doors. Liberation is God's mission.

The second half of the passage reveals the capacity of myth to empower, and the effect of reflection upon myth. The prophet universalizes Genesis 2 to affirm the status of all as children of God. The universal conclusion also restricts any attempt to limit the mission of the servant to any person, even to Jesus. Christ has not become light of the nations because of the scope of his earthly ministry, which was limited to Palestine and essentially to Jews, but because early disciples assumed this passage into their Christology. However, they did not exhaust this passage's possibilities for interpretation. To hear these words in Holy Week one must think not only of Jesus but also of those many servants of God as nameless as this one (cf. Mark 14:3-9), past, present, and yet to come. We too live in an age when what has not been heard in the street has no existence and when democracy means that everyone should enjoy fifteen minutes of fame.

SECOND LESSON

The Epistle to the Hebrews. The author of Hebrews employs images and methods quite unlike those of other NT writers, set forth in a complicated, often convoluted style. Some compare the author to a weaver, others to a composer. These analogies refer to the architectonic structure of the work, with a finely wrought baroque unity that comprehends and integrates a florid variety of themes. One of the difficulties of the work is that the writer approximates, but does not consistently achieve, the learned prose periods of the day and approaches, but does not consistenly work within, the higher intellectual traditions of the time. It may be tempting to wish not to engage this dense and elusive material, but the rewards for those who stay the course are great. The surface appeal of Hebrews during Holy Week is its presentation of Jesus as high priest of a new covenant, a compelling christological model. Perhaps the chief value of Hebrews, however, lies in the freedom it can bestow through its testimony that the great act of redemption cannot be narrowed to a particular concrete scheme. Through a plurality of images blind minds may be opened and imprisoned hearts released.

Lutheran/Common: Hebrews 9:11-15.   The author works with a set of great antitheses contrasting earthly to heavenly, ephemeral to enduring, multiple to singular, new to old. He draws many of his most important symbols from the cultic worship of Israel, viewed in Platonic terms as a fleeting shadow of eternal truth. In accordance with a common ancient view, Hebrews regards the earthly temple as a model of the heavens, and the true heavens as beyond those visible. Through death Christ, whose priesthood is glossed as the source of good things, was exalted into ultimate heaven. The ritual in question is, of course, Yom Kippur. Blood brought together the death of the victim outside of the inner sanctuary with the rite of atonement within. "Blood" is a metaphor, but Jesus did shed his own precious blood. Verses 13-14 continue with an argument from lesser to greater, pursuing the same metaphor of Yom Kippur. The author, like many contemporaries, treats cultic categories morally. Dead bodies pollute. So do "dead" works. Defiled consciences cannot offer worship. In other words, the death of Jesus frees us to serve. These *are* other words, images that can breathe life into dead cliches.

Verse 15 begins a new section, of which it is the summary and thesis. These ideas will receive further development. "New covenant" uses a theme from Jeremiah 31 but does not rest there. The new is opposed to the old and is superior to it. "Covenant" involves a common play upon the Greek word used to render the Hebrew term for "covenant/treaty." The Greek word means "will/testament," and can thus be said to require a death before it becomes effective. Since Christ mediates a new covenant, his atoning death makes our inheritance permanent and sure. The writer of Hebrews would make no distinction between Good Friday and Easter/Ascension and thus provides resources for proclaiming the unity of the Christian Pascha.

Verses 24-28 (included here as part of the Episcopal second lesson on Wednesday) resume the Yom Kippur typology, speaking now of the efficacy of priests rather than victims. Through this means the decisive (for ancients) contrast between the one and the many can be unearthed. In modern terms this means the end of enslavement to our habits and pasts, to the old scenes we replay again and again. This is what cleansing of conscience achieves. The object of transcendent language in ancient idealist philosophy is the human spirit, which is the realm of the "really real." The role of Christ in heaven is not that of presider over a perpetual heavenly liturgy but that of intercessor. Christ's entry into the heavenly tabernacle demonstrates the effectiveness of his self-offering in the spiritual realm of human consciousness. Verse 26 reflects the view of Christ's death as the eschatological event. Verse 27 builds from the commonplace that all die ("death and taxes"), not viewed in accordance with revealed religion but from the popular notion of judgment after death. Death comes but once, so Christ's sacrifice is not to be repeated. This analogy shows the extent of Christ's participation in human nature. His next appearance will be for salvation, not another atonement.

Episcopal: Hebrews 11:39—12:3.   The passage begins with the conclusion to the encomium on fidelity during distress (vv. 32-38). Verse 39 says that, despite the depth and value of their witness, the Hebrew forebears did not obtain the promises. Even these heroes are but shadows of the final goal. God has something even better in mind (v. 40). These verses serve as a brief parenthesis that will stress the final model: none other than faith's perfecter.

Athletic imagery, frequent in ancient literature devoted to the cure of souls, pervades 12:1-3. This is a summons to endure, using Jesus as a paradigm for Christian behavior, for life seen as a marathon rather than a sprint. Athletes laid aside all encumbrances, even their clothes (those crucified were also naked). The "witnesses" are, at one level, spectators of the contest; at another level they are the martyrs, the heroes of faith. The two terms in v. 2, "pioneer and perfecter," play on the sense of beginning and end. The founder is also first to reach the goal (*telos*). Christ is both the model and basis for faith, which is understood here as a quality rather than a statement. The joy Christ experienced after the cross is eschatological bliss. Endurance includes contempt of shame, an attitude uncharacteristic of the ancients. Verse 3 is an invitation coupled with a warning against spiritual weakness that will lead runners to drop out before reaching the finish line.

These verses serve as an exhortation to spiritual fitness, strength, and health. They proclaim that Jesus did not die for the weak to keep us weak, but to open for us new reservoirs and possibilities of strength. If this author can compare the passion to a sporting event, we may begin to search for analogies with which others can find identification.

GOSPEL: JOHN 12:1-11

This Gospel basks in the shadow of the Passion. Among the hints and illusions are a meal with cleansing of feet, a reference to burial, mention of Passover, the presence of resurrected Lazarus, and the emerging treason of Judas. The core is the pronouncement story in verses 1-7 (or 8, which is textually uncertain). The presence of Lazarus, *en famille,* and the appended report in 9-11 tie this scene together with Jesus' resurrection.

Martha follows her confession of faith (11:27) with an act of service (cf. 12:26). Mary anoints Jesus' feet, an act regarded as the most vulgar and luxurious display of conspicuous consumption. The use of her hair for the act bespeaks a devotion both deep and reckless, for women who attended dinners with their hair down were unlikely to enjoy good repute. The odor permeates the home, a vivid witness of its quality and expense, as well as an intimation of the world mission unleashed by Jesus' death (cf. 2 Cor. 2:14 and John 12:20-36). Mary somehow perceives Jesus' message and destiny and responds with unrestrained and extravagant love. She dropped a year's wages on this wasteful gesture. A typical silly woman, some will say, ruled by emotions, reckless with possessions, improvidently prodigal and indulgent. One who evidently would say so is Judas, assigned the objecting role in John, who notifies us that grief over the loss of a potential embezzlement motivated Judas's hypocritical expression of concern for the poor. (The purse in question probably reflects church practice and the frequent questions about the use and misuse of common funds.)

Jesus' mysterious and elliptical reply (a vexation to translators) compels deeper reflection, for she has not preserved the ointment for his burial (and will not appear when two men provide extravagant embalming). One clue may be the recurrent use of "keep" in John with reference to Jesus' word and commandments.

Verses 9-11 testify to the impact of Lazarus' rising and the desperate plans of the authorities to do away with both the source of life and his most conspicuous example. The crowd, which would see and then believe, represent what is for John inadequate faith (20:29). Those who envy Lazarus or any other beneficiaries of Jesus' life-giving power might note that the return to life did not put him on easy street. Like all true disciples, he finds himself endangered.

Here, then, are two models for Holy Week: Judas and Mary. One of them knows very well what is going on and what is prudent. The other does not. There may be a sermon in that.

Episcopal Alternate: Mark 14:3-9. This choice gives opportunity to concentrate upon one segment of the Markan Passion. In Mark this is an interpretive key for the rest of the Gospel. It comes wrapped in plans for deceit and betrayal (vv. 1-2, 10-11). This passage signals the role of women as the only true disciples for the balance of the story. The contrived nature of the objection suggests that an earlier story has been transformed and placed within this context (cf. Luke 7:36-50).

Its power in the present context resides in the portrayal and defense of Christian identity against the objection that the movement's founder died a hideous and criminal death. Jesus' ministry among those rejected—a woman and a leper here—continues. This anonymous individual somehow recognizes and thus accepts his identity. In a prophetic and extravagant act she shatters the perfume jar. We would say that she killed the whole bottle. She anoints not a king, but a potential corpse, performing a beautiful deed for one of the poorest of the poor. Like John 12, this passage makes explicit the understanding of Jesus' death as the source of the world mission. Shattered, he seeks to unite the earth. Jesus' association with sinners was not mere social tolerance. To approve this person and deed was an act of sacramental grace. The one who served received more than she gave.

Tuesday in Holy Week

Lutheran	Roman Catholic	Episcopal	Common Lectionary
Isa. 49:1-6	Isa. 49:1-6	Isa. 49:1-6	Isa. 49:1-7
1 Cor. 1:18-25		1 Cor. 1:18-31	1 Cor 1:18-31
John 12:20-36	John 13:21-33, 36-38	John 12:37-38, 42-50 *or* Mark 11:15-19	John 12:20-36

The various readings reflect upon the nature of revelation and vocation in the light of the redefinitions of wisdom, power, and love that recognition of the offer of salvation to the nations implies.

FIRST LESSON: ISAIAH 49:1-6(7)

The structure is clear enough. In a proclamation addressed to those far off, the servant recounts his call and formation, his mission and its result. His call, which is reminiscent of Jeremiah's, cannot have been based upon accrued merit or proven virtue. The Almighty nurtured and equipped him for his vocation. Each clause of v. 2 begins with the description of an offensive weapon and concludes with assurance of maternal protection. The word will range even to the coastlines and pierce through mighty walls. Verse 3, like other Servant Songs, introduces a regal note: The prophet is acclaimed like a king. ("Israel" here contradicts v. 5, where the servant is sent to Israel, and is thus a later gloss, indicating the antiquity of the corporate interpretation of the role.) The servant's report in v. 4 interrupts the flow of encouraging news. He believes that his mission was a disaster. The expression of failure is no less frank than his assurance of divine support is sure.

The power of this passage lies in its vagueness. We also have a vocation beyond the bounds of womb and tomb and have been fitted out with the armor of salvation. We, too, have often lamented the futility of our labor. Do we also express unswerving trust in God? God takes a different view of the weak and the foolish. After a reiteration of the original call in v. 5, including a nice play on "bring back," the Most High requests a supplement. Saving the chosen people is "too light a thing." Such missions were perfectly suited to national gods whose stock went up with their clients' political prestige, but this God has in view something more significant: light to the nations. The armor of light is somehow different from military belt buckles inscribed *"Gott mit uns"* or nuclear submarines named *Corpus Christi.*

To appreciate the revolutionary force of these verses one should note that in a polytheistic environment people presumed that when the going got tough, weak gods got going, usually toward captivity in the temples of the victor, and, furthermore, that shame was a form and mark of suffering in the ancient world. Those shamed were to be shunned. The light of God which the servant is to proclaim is faithfulness rather than might, a light glowing in the darkness of shame, even the shame of the cross.

SECOND LESSON: 1 CORINTHIANS 1:18-25(31)

What does an instrument of shame have to do with money/status, power, and success? Some of the more prominent Christians at Corinth had aspirations to upward mobility and were not interested in stressing some of the less respectable aspects of the origins of their new religion. Power they could appreciate, and its handmaid, education. One way to help the young faith and themselves up the social ladder was to progress from the elementary language of the creed to new and enlightening insights. Paul begs to differ, and does so with rhetorical sophistication and penetrating insight of his own.

None of his audience would dispute God as the origin and standard for wisdom and the source of all power, nor the difference between heavenly truth and earthly illusion. The apostle brilliantly exploits these shared values to set forth the cross as criterion for Christian theology. The message of the cross is not a kind of primer for the "weak," to be supplemented by the wisdom of the "strong." If divine power emerges in what humans find miraculous, then Jesus should have taken the dare to show how he could leap down from the pinnacle of the cross.

As the benchmark for wisdom and definition of power, the scandal of the cross continues to sting. To treat this as a piece of anti-intellectual diatribe would miss the point. Paul uses wisdom. To speculate about racial characteristics will also lead interpretation astray. There were, and are, many Jews, Greeks, and, for that matter, "barbarians," with no small interest in both wisdom and power. These groups stand for various efforts to verify and thereby manipulate the divine. The apparently powerless shame of the cross has in fact wrought the miracle of unity for the human race—or should have—unity being one miracle in scant supply just then. For those who lust after social advancement Paul recommends a demographic survey, the results of which he anticipates. Facts are revealing.

The fact of the cross is God's primary revelation and the rule by which every notion of power and each definition must be measured. The one crucified is the Wisdom of God and the power of God: point, game, set, and match. But we do not easily get the point and games go on, within ourselves, our communities, our nation, and our world.

GOSPEL

Lutheran/Common: John 12:20-36. Immediately following Jesus' strangely regal entry in the world center of revealed religion, the city where he will die, some Gentiles appear, foreshadowing the later world mission. The "Jews" evaluated in John 12 *have* sought signs but have been blind to their manifestation. Ironically, these Greeks seek neither wisdom nor signs, but are open questers for the water of life. Verses 21-22 show this by evoking 1:35-51, the call of the first disciples. For Jesus these seekers are a sign of his "hour," the passion in which he will be lifted up to draw all to himself, the death that will plant the seed of life (cf. the parables of Mark 4 and 1 Cor. 15:37). The association shifts in v. 25, a Johannine reflex of Mark 8:34-35, less paradoxical because the tense is present. Those who cherish survival will live in continuous death, while eternal life begins now and endures.

Verses 27-28 resemble Gethsemane, but differ because Jesus need not pray "your will not mine," for he and the Father are one in will. The notion of rescue appears only as a rhetorical absurdity. Glory, however, is invoked. Conventional thinking would locate glorification in precisely the rescue of Jesus from death. In John glory is the victory of God's will through the revelation of Jesus' self-oblation rather than the gratification of last-second amelioration. This petition receives a reply, a "voice," experienced elsewhere in the gospel tradition at such moments as the baptism and the transfiguration. For many in the crowd the endorsement was mere noise. The superstitious have long been wont to regard thunder and lightning as revelatory, to be sure, but John has more in mind than an illustration from the religio-historical repertory of sky gods. All signs are ambiguous, and naturalistic explanations or appeals to coincidence lie always at hand.

Jesus interrupts the dispute with an important announcement: The long-awaited apocalyptic turn of the ages is now taking place, for the great enemy has lost grip on the world and the savior is ascending into heaven with humanity in tow. Now devotees of apocalypses would find this a trifle overstated, since the incidents in question are to be highly palpable and quite decisive. There should be no question when the end has come. Our evangelist interjects a comment in v. 33, a bold piece of Johannine reinterpretation of tradition. The new age will have its birthplace on Golgotha, and Jesus rather than drawing souls into heaven calls persons to follow him to rejection and shame (v. 26). The Son of Man ascends on a cross rather than a cloud. To "take up" believers is to remove them from the realm of darkness, which happens when Satan is expelled from the microcosm of their lives. Two emphatic "nows" drive these nails home.

The crowd measures all this by conventional wisdom and finds it foolishly wanting. They presume the messiah they get will be the one they want, and they do not want one who will go away and leave them comfortless. Jesus presses on with undaunted exhortation, pushing the images of darkness and light. Access to the latter is not unlimited. Revelation is not a perpetual lamp.

His final words are an invitation to the life-giving light that beams from the paschal source of the cross. Those who hold that lamp to their feet will not stumble.

Roman Catholic: John 13:21-33, 36-38.   (For the structure of John 13, see the discussion of the Gospel for Holy Thursday.) The theme of this passage is betrayal. At the core of the Synoptic-like traditions is a saying about a traitor, shaped in accordance with the psalms of individual lament. The Fourth Evangelist develops this tradition in characteristic ways. Verse 21 resumes the subject introduced in vv. 18-19, establishing a link with the interpretation of the footwashing. Rather than grieved, as in the Synoptics, the disciples here, as usual, are perplexed. Help is sought by Peter from a source first mentioned at this point, in the course of Jesus' revelation to his intimates. The Beloved Disciple is an anonymous figure who holds a privileged position, both at dinner, beside Jesus, and in the text, where he alone knows and perceives what transpires. Because he has no name, the Beloved Disciple serves as one with whom the implied reader may identify.

None of the others hear the interchange among the Beloved Disciple, Jesus, and Judas. Betrayal remains cloaked in obscurity. The means of identification is a quasi-sacramental act. Judas receives Satan. Eucharistic theology informs this passage, and vice-versa. As master of even his own betrayal, Jesus directs Judas to leave. The call for haste comes not from a "let's get the worst over as soon as possible" attitude, but from his clarity of vocational purpose.

Attention shifts to the disciples' conjectures about the reasons for Judas' untimely exit, ironically evoking 12:1-11, with its judgment about Judas' views on the poor and its description of the anointing of Jesus' feet in anticipation of burial. The shadow of the Passion falls, deepening in v.

30, when Judas gobbles down his morsel and dashes out. This is no Passover meal, but it does contain a parody of the rubrics for that meal (Exod. 12:11), acted out by one on his way to hand the Paschal Lamb over to the slaughterers.

The simplest of phrases serves to end this poignant narrative: "It was night." One might, of course, find here a chronological note for those who want the times so that they can record Holy Week on their VCRs without missing their favorite shows. Another possibility is the night when no one can work (9:4). Night is specifically the time of the Passion and thus generally a mode of existence. John requires no legend about Judas' death. He has left the fellowship and entered the realm of darkness. Holy Week preachers might take note of how much can be said, to those with ears cultivated for hearing, in seven Greek or ten Roman letters.

Jesus jolts us by selecting this moment to hail the arrival of divine glory (vv. 31-32). The betrayal is a synecdoche for the entire Passion, which is seen as glorious revelation. Traditional views like to reserve this notion for the final coming "in power and great glory." This evangelist is not traditional and sees glory shining in the apparent darkness of the cross. Revelation is obedience taking the form of service. What is, by secular standards, called "shame" is here pronounced to be glory.

The logic of v. 33 builds from the identification of Jesus' glorification with his death/departure. On the surface the problem is his physical whereabouts. When considered in depth (John 14–16), it is the situation of the post-Easter community that is in mind. The announcement of Jesus' departure sets the stage for the prediction of Peter's denial. Not understanding, he protests with genuine love clouded by blindness. The reader's knowledge of his eventual fate produces irony. Jesus ruthlessly crushes his objections with the assertion that he will deny him three times that night. He has the last word.

Peter and Judas are the characters who illustrate the themes of love and betrayal. Peter loves but does not grasp what love requires. He wants to have Jesus all the time. This is not contemptible, but it would deny the need for Jesus' death and departure and the true character of discipleship. Love is more than sentiment. Judas, on the other hand, represents love for the world, of which money is the primary symbol. For us the situation of Peter seems to raise a deeper challenge: love that leads to betrayal.

Episcopal: John 12:37-38, 42-50. The closing portion of the first part of the Fourth Gospel offers a retrospective upon Jesus' public mission. Verse 37 flatly defines the "signs" as a failure. They were popular enough, but attracted those who wished to see wonders rather than signs pointing beyond themselves. Verse 38 shows that this failure accords with revelation. The recommended omission of vv. 39-40 is unfortunate, for it is part of what amounts to a summary of John 9.

The most advanced form of Johannine Christology emerges in v. 41, which applies the glory seen by Isaiah (6:1) to Christ (cf. John 17:5). The analysis is thus theological rather than historical and does not report irrevocable decrees of divine fate. As if this were not exegetical vexation enough, vv. 42-43 return to and clash with v. 37! The evangelist does not like fence sitters who wished to maintain the social and religious benefits of synagogue membership by concealing their acknowledgment of Christ. Verse 43 points toward a broader application of this judgment about a problem that is not historically limited. The essence of unbelief is self-seeking (human glory). The essence of belief is self-giving (divine glory as revealed by Jesus).

Blindness is ultimately inability to see beyond one's self-interest. These verses should be applied in ways that look beyond Christian self-justification to call for a self-examination that recognizes the tragic results of our own, and others', blindnesses.

Since the withdrawal recorded in v. 36b seemed final, vv. 44-50 come as a surprise. They probably represent a later addition and are a theological mix of early and later concepts. The mixture thus comprehends the range of Johannine traditions, while the renewal of Jesus' message after the apparently ultimate evaluation serves to remind us that revelation can take the form of "no," but that no is never the final word. Jesus, like Wisdom personified, cries out for the last time in public, adding a final invitation to life. If there is apologetic here, there is also the affirmation that no human means can validate Jesus' claims. Revelation submits to no tests. Verses 44-45 assert that those who see Jesus have seen the One who sent him. Is this all there is? What notion of deity does this infer? Still, one is not to confuse the sender with the one who is sent, a point well taken when really heard by clergy and people. If darkness results, Jesus would not have it, for he would be light and liberate all from that which threatens to engulf them (v. 46). Verses 47-48 assert that judgment resides in response to the message, not from outside. The passage ends with Jesus' statement that he did not speak out of his own issues, needs, or beliefs. This is all the "proof" he will offer. The ultimate "summary of the law" is not even "love your neighbor." It is light and life eternal.

Episcopal Alternate: Mark 11:15-19. This offers splendid opportunities for the courageous. The Markan "cleansing of the Temple" is really a closing, for Jesus prevents all cultic activity. Three of the most important clues to its interpretation are, in inverse order of importance: 1. The term "robbers" (for the significance see the discussion of Mark 15:27, above). 2. The close parallels in this episode to the parable in 3:27. Jesus has entered the house of the strong man and bound him. 3. The incident is inserted into the midst of the strange tale of the fate of the fig tree: Jesus has "cursed" the Temple and it will die.

The effect of this selection is to interrupt our pious meditations about the tragic death of innocent Jesus with an important announcement that Jesus of Nazareth has just disrupted the center of the universe and the locus of revealed faith with a terrorist attack. Holy Week strips away our defenses one by one until we face only naked and ominous realities. One of these realities is to imagine that Jesus was a good guy who told nice stories and was put to death by villains too warped by evil to recognize their own self-interest. The Passion is not a soap opera, no, not even the prototype of the television miniseries. There is more than one way to blunt the scandal and mask the folly of the cross.

Wednesday in Holy Week

Lutheran	Roman Catholic	Episcopal	Common Lectionary
Isa. 50:4-9a	Isa. 50:4-9	Isa. 50:4-9a	Isa. 50:4-9a
Rom. 5:6-11		Heb. 9:11-15, 24-28	Heb. 12:1-3
Matt. 26:14-25	Matt. 26:14-25	John 13:31-35 *or* Matt 26:1-5, 14-25	John 13:21-30

FIRST LESSON: ISAIAH 50:4-9(a)

For discussion of this text please refer to its treatment under the first reading for Palm Sunday, above.

SECOND LESSON

Lutheran: Romans 5:6-11.   After his scriptural arguments in support of justification by faith, Paul begins to unfold his understanding of the concept. Like reconciliation, with which it is more or less comparable, justification is not a mere state. It is the revelation and operation of divine power.

Verses 6-8 have a closely knit structure built around the phrase "Christ died for us while we were weak/sinners." "Sinners" refers to human status before God; "weak" to its anthropological result. The first of the intervening phrases contains almost playful speculation about what sort of person one might die for, the effect of which is to magnify the beneficence of Jesus' death. The point is then driven home with a rapid thrust: The act has nothing to do with nobility but with God's enduring love.

The two subsequent verses continue with arguments from lesser to greater. The reconciliation experienced in and the hope established by baptism are the down payments for eschatological bliss. "Life" in v. 10 does not refer to the deeds of the "historical" Jesus, including his death. As in 2 Cor. 4:10-18—perhaps the best commentary—life, too, is that power which forms and preserves the community, now and forever. Verse 11 returns to a theme stated in v. 3: "boasting." Its antonym is "shame," specifically the shame of the cross; its effect is paradoxical.

Jesus not only died for sinners, but also ate and drank with them, even with traitors, and thereby both modeled and effected reconciliation. Others may now do the same, if they accept God's offer and see that the cross empowers us to root out that estrangement which is endemic to the world. God's love is always a transitive verb.

Episcopal: Hebrews 9:11-15, 24-28. See under the second lesson for Monday in Holy Week.

Common: Hebrews 12:1-3. See the Episcopal second lesson for Monday in Holy Week.

GOSPEL

Lutheran/Roman Catholic/Episcopal Alternate: Matthew 26:(1-5)14-25.
This selection provides the perspective of another evangelist upon the course and meaning of Jesus' death. In verses 1-5 Matthew opens with two brief scenes that provide a dramatic introduction, first with a solemn "fourth prediction of the Passion" by Jesus to his disciples, then with a report of the equally solemn resolution of the "chief priests and elders of the people" to trap and execute him. Two parties pursue the same ends for different motives. The victim alone knows the correct time, Passover. Is the celebration of deliverance from death an appropriate occasion for murder plots? We know that actual deliverance will occur. As if to avoid these connotations, the leaders speak only of "the feast," which for them is inpropitious. The plotters do not know when Jesus will actually die! Their brief speech, vividly given in direct discourse, also shows that the people stand with Jesus against the authorities and serves to raise suspense through retardation. Will these officials find their opportunity?

Verses 14-25. This lection forms a tryptich: *A.* Judas' plans to deliver Jesus up (vv. 14-16). *B.* Preparation to keep the feast (v. 17-19). *A.* Prediction of Judas' betrayal (vv. 20-25).

A. The "then" of v. 14 links the action of Judas with that of the leaders (v. 3). The Matthean scene is vivid, with direct speech, the suggestion of greed as a motive, and the presence of unconscious prophecy. The stipulated price is the traditional cost of a slave (Exod. 21:32) and the wages of a shepherd (Zech. 11:4-14). The irony is delicious, revealing the blindness of both parties: Judas by greed, the leaders by fear and envy. It also foreshadows 27:3-10. Judas is the first disciple to depart. One who had left all to follow Jesus leaves him in quest of gain.

B. Whereas the preceding is longer than Mark, Matthew's account of the preparation for Passover is shorter. Gone is the parallel to the preparation for entering Jerusalem. The disciples take the initiative. Their behavior contrasts with that of Judas, a point underscored by use of the same verb in vv. 15 and 17. Jesus' reply displays his sovereign control: "My *kairos* is near," a reflection of v. 2 and a contrast with the *eukairia* sought by

Judas in v. 16. He is to be betrayed but will nonetheless keep the feast, for it will bring deliverance. The divine plan unfolds with quickness and precision amidst growing horror.

A. This horror bursts forth from the disciples when Jesus introduces the subject of betrayal from among his intimates. They rather childishly seek individual reassurance of nonresponsibility. In Matthew, v. 23 applies to a specific individual and works like a divinatory response. Verse 24 explains 18:7. Judas offers the opening and closing words of the triptych. How are we to understand his motives? The essence of betrayal is the desire for self-protection. "Rabbi" is the very word he will use at the moment of betrayal, with an act even more intimate than the sharing of a dish (v. 49). Jesus' reply, almost identical to his response to the question of Pilate (27:11), is ambiguous. "Whatever you have said, Judas." Judas said it all in his question to the high priests.

Proclamation of this Gospel will not succeed if it gives the people a villain to excoriate with a sense of superiority and relief. Everybody in this scene raises the question of self. Matthew, like the other evangelists, links betrayal to love. More recent instances of betrayal from within may come to mind. The goal, however, is not to exacerbate paralyzing guilt through remorse but to empower one another with the courage to set our faces like flint and to endure through the power of faith.

Episcopal: John 13:31-35. For the setting and a discussion of verses 31-33 see under the Roman Catholic Gospel for Tuesday in Holy Week.

The problem of Jesus' departure, discussed at length in John 14 and 16, generated conflict, one result of which was the insertion of vv. 34-35 at this point, disrupting the connection between vv. 33 and 36. Few regret this famous interpolation, but it does require reflection and, to a degree, supplementation. In what sense can the command be called "new"? Surely the idea is both old and widespread. Is this Johannine "summary of the law" a situation ethic, a general humanitarian slogan, or a sentimental concept? Each of these paths has been explored, and not always with happy results.

This "new" has nothing to do with novelty. It is rather the eschatological gift of new creation, from the One who makes all things new. Love is thus the eschatological gift which determines the pastoral constitution of the community. What Jesus gives is not a suggestion for living but the possibility of obeying an old command. He reveals how to walk in newness of life. The indicative of his gift ("I loved") makes the imperative a new and exciting possibility. Verse 34 thus serves as a summary comment upon

13:12-20. It further states (with reinforcement in vv. 36-38) that Jesus is not to be an object of love, that believers are not to point their love toward him in a personal relationship but that, since he is absent, they must share with other members of the community what they have gained from him. Verse 35, like 1 Corinthians 13, views this behavior as the one authenticating Christian credential.

This is all well and good, but as a basis for contemporary Christian ethics it is not adequate. Within the context of a small, beleaguered community it has merit, not least for minority groups who cannot exhaust their energy reassuring the majority. Nor is there any reason to regret the particular depth and quality of intracommunity love. Nonetheless, for the majority of Christians in North America, the love received from Christ is properly extended beyond community borders. The intensity of Christians' internal focus during Holy Week is necessary and appropriate, but it must, as the solemn collects of Good Friday direct, become a source of strength for reaching out our arms in love to all whom Christ would embrace.

Common: John 13:21-30. See the Roman Catholic Gospel for Tuesday in Holy Week.

Maundy/Holy Thursday

Lutheran	Roman Catholic	Episcopal	Common Lectionary
Exod. 24:3-11	Exod. 12:1-8, 11-14	Exod. 12:1-14a	Exod. 12:1-14 or Exod. 24:3-8
1 Cor. 10:16-17	1 Cor. 11:23-26	1 Cor. 11:23-26 (27-32)	1 Cor. 11:23-26 or 1 Cor 10:16-17
Mark 14:12-26	John 13:1-15	John 13:1-15 or Luke 22:14-30	John 13:1-15 or Mark 14:12-26

The particular function of the readings on this occasion is to explain what Christians are about, with particular emphasis upon the constitutive character of the Eucharist and its origin in connection with Jesus' death and resurrection. Both the Lutheran and the Roman Catholic/Episcopal propers deal with Passover and eucharistic origins, although in different ways.

The Lutheran first reading coordinates with the Gospel and gives the context of Jesus' death as a sacrifice establishing the New Covenant. The Gospel relates the origin of the Eucharist in a Passover Meal. The Roman Catholic/Episcopal scheme devotes the first lesson to the directions for Passover, the second to Paul's account of the institution of the Eucharist, and the Gospel to the ceremony of footwashing. On Maundy/Holy Thursday the Church focuses upon the Eucharist as the re-creation of a historical redemption with roots in the Israelite tradition, as an act connected with Jesus' ministry, and epitomized in his Passion, and, finally, as the force which sustains his community of care and love. With the evening liturgy begins the great and sacred three days of worship encompassing the Pascha of our God.

(Although the Common Lectionary permits any of the choices from the Lutheran or Roman Catholic/Episcopal readings, those who employ this lectionary would do well to ascertain that their choices permit at least two of the major themes to appear: Passover, Institution of the Eucharist, or "Maundy" rite. Because of the options, no specific references to this lectionary will occur below.)

FIRST LESSON

Lutheran: Exodus 24:3-11. The merger of two sources has yielded a rich harvest. Verses 9-11 complete vv. 1-2, and report a covenant banquet after a manifestation. "They beheld God, and they ate and drank" (11b). Verses 3-8, on the other hand, reflect the covenant renewal ceremony, including a reading of the text, verbal assent, and a sacrifice with the use of blood.

The covenant ceremony views Moses as a mediator. There is no official priesthood, so youths perform the sacrifice. Does the blood bind together people and God (symbolized by the altar), or is it a symbol of communion of life, or a purificatory rite? Perhaps it shows the people bound by blood and God as manifesting mercy. The ceremony may strike us as crude, but its power is unmistakable and its meaning not easily tucked into a single envelope. No less crude and beautiful is the following theophany, described more boldly than in Isaiah 6:1. Only the platform beneath God's feet receives a description. It is transparent and made of lapis lazuli, which, with its blue hue and golden flecks, would mirror the heavens. Beneath this model of the celestial vault they ate and drank safely in the presence of the Almighty! A kindred idea inspired architects of a later age to build baldachins with gold stars on a blue field over the altars of Christian churches.

Blood seals a covenant that the people have ratified. Jesus' blood also binds together heaven and earth in a covenant ratified by our "Amen." Through blending these two sources the author juxtaposes two different pictures: the covenant ceremony and a banquet in which select representatives sit at the high table. These two themes have endured in eucharistic theology with its stresses both upon the sacrifice of Christ and the festival banquet. "They beheld God, and they ate and drank." So do we, but not without danger, Paul will insist.

Roman Catholic/Episcopal: Exodus 12:1-14(a). All of this material is from the priestly source. Verses 1-13 deal with preparation for Passover; 14-20 with the Feast of Unleavened Bread. Cultic practice has shaped the account. These directions do not match our expectations for a banquet of liberation. The meal does include one yearling kid or lamb and we're off to a good start, but roasting it whole, head, shins, and entrails, and serving it up with unleavened bread and bitter herbs represent something of a decline. Bitter herbs were all that was available in early spring, and unleavened bread was the only kind that could be whipped up without an overnight wait for dough to rise. As for the entree, it was the kind of meat one could have time to drain but not to butcher. This is a scratch meal, hastily prepared. And even more hastily eaten, not in formals but dressed for the road with overcoats on and boots zipped up. If we may presume that God does not regard truck stops as repositories of heavenly cuisine, we should say that this meal resembles nothing so much as the furtive munching of a bunch of fugitives grabbing a bite to fortify them for the beckoning road. To be sure, there was some decoration, a rich coat of fresh blood on every door, but even this was more utilitarian than ornamental.

We, too, gather in communities confronted by an indifferent or hostile world. We, too, are but wanderers and pilgrims in this life. We, too, must be affected by a sense of urgency and itinerancy if our eucharists and vocations are taken with some gravity. The ancient Hebrews had already wrested these festivals from their primitive connection with natural cycles and framed them to teach about God's times and seasons. Every communion is, in some sense, the *viaticum,* bread for the road, or as a still popular old hymn put it: *"O Esca Viatorum,"* "O bread to pilgrims given." Sometimes the Hebrew Bible interprets the New Testament.

SECOND LESSON

Lutheran: 1 Corinthians 10:16-17.   First Cor. 10:1-22 presents a discourse on sacramental theology, beginning with reference to the events of the exodus. Although Paul will grant in principle the freedom to eat meat sacrificed to idols (chap. 8), he will not condone participation in actual pagan worship. The experience of the wilderness generation shows that those liberated from bondage then fed with supernatural sustenance had no guarantee. The sacraments are not magical amulets that free recipients from the consequences of their behavior. They free and empower believers for love.

In verses 14-22 Paul uses sacramental life and action as the ground for avoiding other worship. All agree that the Eucharist is a corporate act which creates community. The apostle deploys this understanding to interpret ecclesiology in terms of sacramental theology. Communion is less an act of individual piety and private edification than the act that always forms the Body of Christ. Because he wishes to exploit the symbol of the single loaf, Paul refers first to the cup. *Koinonia* ("sharing") is a rich word, for it includes the concept of a common life and the sharing of possessions, qualities notable at Corinth for nonobservance. Paul plays with "Body of Christ" as referring to either church or sacrament. He insists that it means both and that participation in the Eucharist rules other options out. We are what we eat.

Roman Catholic/Episcopal: 1 Corinthians 11:23-26(32).   Understanding of this famous passage requires some attention to the context. After the discussion of various matters dealing with worship and life, Paul begins to engage some Corinthian practices directly, first by taking up the letter's opening theme: the role of groups and factions. Apparently the relatively wealthy (the backbone of "the strong") conducted the celebration with little regard for the "weak" and poor. In control of their own schedules and disposing of adequate resources, the wealthier could arrive early, occupy the few couches available in the houses of their equally comfortable friends and leaders of house-based assemblies, and party all evening. Poor and slave would drift in when finished with or released from their labors, having meager supplies or none, to find seating on the floor or in the courtyard as best they could. Paul asserts that this is a private *(idion)* party, not the Dominical *(kyriakon)* Banquet. The Lord's Supper demands sharing, opposing the notion of the personal to the communal. The Eucharist creates equality. Verses 18-20 presuppose that when the community gathers, it celebrates the Eucharist. Within this framework Paul appeals to the "institution narrative," a known element of the tradition he can evoke to support his critique.

Verse 23 opens with technical terms for the transmission of tradition. This material is pre-Pauline. (The claim that he received it "from the Lord" asserts divine authorization of his apostleship rather than the immediate source.) As in Mark 14 and its parallels, the account presumes the Jewish practice of pronouncing blessings, prayers of thanks and praise, over various items of food. The prominent features of this account are the words given to interpret the ordinary action.

There are important differences from Mark: 1. There is no specification of a Passover setting. 2. Paul uses the more or less synonymous "give thanks," rather than "bless." 3. There is no mention of giving or taking the foods. 4. The term "body" is glossed with "for you." 5. The action over each is enjoined as a "remembrance" of Jesus. 6. The cup is not equated with "blood," but as "the *new* Covenant *in my blood.*"

Paul grounds the action within the earthly life of Jesus and ties it to his death (rather than, for example, to a heavenly repast or miraculous feeding). "For you" introduces the concept of sacrifice that removes sins. "In remembrance" is not an invitation to sentimental recollection or to nostalgia, but is a means for making past saving acts present and effective for the community, as the "memorial acclamations" of the liturgies emphasize.

The apostle's specific interpretation of "remembrance" emerges in v. 26. The Eucharist includes and implies the proclamation of Jesus' death, of his full human life offered in service to others. This is worth remembering on Maundy Thursday. "Until he comes" restricts the rite to the life of the church on earth. Paul would stifle any identification of the Eucharist as a messianic banquet because of the problems manifested at Corinth when some began to pretend that they were living in heaven. That the cup is equated with "covenant" rather than with "blood" does indeed indicate that Paul's account is less rounded than Mark's and that bread was the more important of the two elements. It also appeals directly to Jeremiah 31 and makes covenant a primary rather than a secondary quality of remembrance and presence. Exodus 24, rather than Exodus 12, is in view.

The following (vv. 27-32) injunctions to careful preparation and self-examination may strike us as unwelcome reminders of the communion pieties liturgical renewal has attempted to modify. These commands are not, however, individualistic in thrust. Paul keeps his gaze upon the entire community. The "body" to which v. 29 applies is first and foremost the church. Those nourished with the sacrament are to have their eyes opened to glimpse the real presence of their Savior in their brothers and sisters. Discerning the body means engaging in research and reflection about community needs.

GOSPEL

Lutheran: Mark 14:12-26.   There are three scenes: preparation for Passover (vv. 12-17), prediction of betrayal (vv. 18-21), and meal (vv. 22-25), the central one of which deals with betrayal. Eating with Jesus is the theme of the entire passage, appropriately enough for the occasion.

Verses 10-11 and 12-17 set forth two plans: Jesus' for Passover, the chief priests' for murder. Their plans smack of opportunism and caution; his plans march on in majesty. The preparation for Passover resembles 11:2-6, preparation for the entry, and links the two: Both Jerusalem and Passover have become ambiguous symbols. First Samuel 10:1-16 should be consulted for theme and motifs. The fairy-tale quality of the incident shows that God is in control, appearances notwithstanding. A man carrying a water jar would stand out. A woman brought a jar to Jesus at v. 3. From now on the roles are reversed: women are the true disciples. The orders for preparation make the subsequent dinner a Passover meal. This is probably a Markan contribution to the tradition, as the following scenes do not contain Passover practices.

Verses 18-21 establish that eating with Jesus means the acceptance of betrayal, even death. One cannot truly eat with him if unwilling to share his fate. This is Markan eucharistic theology. Betrayal is a theological condition, like blindness. The course the Son of Man will follow is determined, but divine sovereignty does not abrogate human responsibility.

Formally, vv. 22-25 are etiological, a story explaining what we do. Liturgical practice had already shaped the narrative, as indicated by the fourfold "take, bless, break, share," and the brevity of the commands. In Mark this is an implicit warrant for eucharistic practice and meaning. All eucharistic theologies are interpretations of Jesus' mission; Mark's eucharistic theology is characteristically embedded in the Passion. Bread is a profound symbol of Jesus' self and ministry. This is the final meal in Mark, the third major meal story, following the feedings of 6:30-44 and 8:1-10, of which it is the climax and interpretation. The focus is upon Jesus' absence. There is no injunction to "remembrance." Verse 25 opens with a solemn "truly." "Until" is a proleptic cry of hope, of the certainty that he will drink again (cf. 1 Cor. 11:26). This refers to the messianic banquet, from which the ceremony just described is distinguished. An effect of the verse is to make the scene a pronouncement story, with the climax at v. 25.

The "Institution Narrative" reveals three levels of meaning: 1. "This is . . .": sacramental communion. 2. The death of Jesus as a sacrifice establishing the covenant (cf. Exod. 24:3-11). 3. "For many" (which means for all; cf. Isa. 53:12; Mark 10:45): Jesus' death is the saving event. Number one is primary. Mark gives special emphasis to the cup and uses these words to express his theology (cf. 10:38; 14:36).

The statement that "they all drank" is not a command, as in Matthew. It shows their unwitting participation in Jesus' fate (cf. 14:36). The supper scene is a powerful theological reflection upon the death of Jesus. Through his giving of himself he summons and nourishes the many nameless ones. The Passover setting provides more than irony, for it proclaims that those who eat this meal commit themselves to the liberation of the oppressed. Already by the time of the earliest Gospel the Eucharist was a multivalent rite with several layers of meaning.

Roman Catholic/Episcopal: John 13:1-15. At chap. 13 the Gospel shifts from public proclamation to Jesus' revelation to his own people, a transition emphasized in 13:1. The focus is upon the remaining followers, a group not limited to the Twelve and including the mysterious "Beloved Disciple," whose insight permits informed readers to understand. The language of chaps. 13–17 becomes increasingly more enigmatic, despite its directness and repetition. There are said to be two types of poets: Those who seek in their various works to absorb the entire language like a sponge, embracing all its words, and those who seek to use fewer and fewer words with more and more meaning. By analogy, the Fourth Evangelist belongs to the second group.

Narrative dominates chap. 13. The setting is somewhat like the Synoptics: final meal, prediction of betrayal, and the one who betrays. For John this is not a Passover meal, nor does it report the institution of the Eucharist. These differences may well be more primitive, but the evangelist develops them in the service of his own theology.

This simple scheme seeks to illuminate the structure and method:

Verses	Subject	Theme	Central Character(s)
A. 1-3	Introduction	Love/Betrayal	
B. 4-20	Washing and interpretations	Love	Peter
C. 21-30	Announcement of traitor	Betrayal	Beloved Disciple/Judas
D. 31-35	Absence and New Commandment	Love	Community
E. 36-38	Denial	Betrayal	Peter

Verses 1-3 introduce the balance of the Gospel, for the "hour" is the occasion of Jesus' return to God, not the Parousia. World and God are less entries upon a cosmographic chart than realms of power and types of existence. This would be a suitable preface to a glorious ascension until the words "the Devil had already put it into the heart of Judas. . . ." On the feast of deliverance the redeemer will be sold down the river.

Verse 4 begins well enough, as Jesus rises from the table, presumably for an address suitable to the occasion. Then he begins to undress, a second ominous note. His next disrobing will be involuntary. Then, properly clad for the task, the master begins to wash his pupils' feet, the lord acting like a slave, and the laws of nature have been irretrievably breached. We do believe that in the Eucharist fundamental laws do come tumbling down, that heaven and earth briefly meet, but it is a bit disconcerting to meet this breach in the washing of feet. Since the ancients wore sandals on dirt roads coated with the emission products of natural vehicles, footwashing was the most unpleasant and servile of tasks. The dissonance of these few verses embraces and encapsulates the entire paradox of the Johannine Passion.

Two disparate interpretations of the action follow. The first, in vv. 6-11, presents the action as a symbol of Jesus' humble service for others. The second, in vv. 12-20, offers the action as an example of how believers should serve one another. Together they constitute the indicative and imperative of Christian ethics. Because Jesus has washed us, we can serve one another.

Peter takes the lead in this typical bit of Johannine misunderstanding. His reaction reveals not just personal discomfort with being served, but dismay about the implications for leadership of what Jesus has done. Christologically, what Jesus has done is enough. (There is probably reference to baptism here.) This service does not convey immunity. Judas will soon make his exit with tidy feet. It brings neither security nor status.

Status is an issue, but not the primary one. Leadership must take the form of service. There is another servile experience in store for Jesus: Death on the cross, and that is the apex of revelation. In this Gospel revelation is a gift that takes the form of service (cf. also 12:1-8). The lectionary selection ends on a dramatic note, stressing the example to be imitated.

The earliest attestation of liturgical imitation of the washing of feet comes from Milan, in the fourth century, when the New Testament became a source for rituals of historical reenactment. The Gospel should remain in control, for the purpose is not self-abasement, but symbolized discipleship. In the context of Exodus 12 we may say that on this festival of freedom leaders are freed to act like servants and all invited to sit down freely together at table to eat the bread of angels, a splendid but ominous dish, purchased at great price and bringing alarming benefits. Those who wish a quick trip had better leave with Judas. Those who want heavenly bread to procure safety might note that *this* Passover will not protect even the first-born of God from dreadful harm. What are its benefits? Well, those who eat it can wash one another's feet, feet needed for the journey, feet washed first by Christ and made beautiful through proclamation of good news. In the *corpus Christi* the head cannot say to the feet "I do not need you." So we must eat and get on our feet. An appointment awaits us in a garden.

Episcopal Alternate: Luke 22:14-30. This option is presumably intended for liturgies which will make no use of the "Maundy" rite. Luke is close to John 13:12-20, for the Christology is exemplarist and based upon the model of service. Mark 10:40-45 finds its Lukan equivalent in this setting. Luke does not present the death of Jesus as an atoning sacrifice, and his eucharistic theology corresponds. (Despite the reading of the New RSV, vv. 19b-20 remain suspect.) Leadership means service, of which the Eucharist, in which the leaders prepare and serve the meal, is the model. In Luke's Gospel Jesus continues his ministry of service even on the cross and is truly in our midst as one who serves.

Good Friday

Lutheran	Roman Catholic	Episcopal	Common Lectionary
Isa. 52:13—53:12	Isa. 52:13—53:12	Isa. 52:13—53:12 *or* Gen. 22:1-18 *or* Wis. 2:1,12-24	Isa. 52:13—53:12
Heb. 4:14-16; 5:7-9	Heb. 4:14-16; 5:7-9	Heb. 10:1-25	Heb. 4:14-16, 5:7-9
John 18:1—19:42	John 18:1—19:42	John 18:1—19:42 *or* 19:1-37	John 18:1—19:42 *or* 19:17-30

These propers set forth the understanding that the Good Friday liturgy is not a requiem for Jesus but a restrained and solemn exposition of the triumph of the cross and thus a celebration of the paschal mystery in its fullness. In the words of the anthem used since the Middle Ages:

> We glory in your cross, O Lord,
> And praise and glorify your holy resurrection.
> For by virtue of your cross
> Joy has come to the whole world.

FIRST LESSON: ISAIAH 52:13—53:12

Whereas the psalm of individual lament had provided formal shape to other Servant Songs, the content of 53:1-11a shows affinities with the individual psalm of thanksgiving. The narration is in third person rather than first. The servant's delivery is celebrated by others, for in his vindication they, too, found salvation. Their report also contains an admission that their judgment had proved erroneous. They found the servant ugly. Beauty, virtue, and strength were believed to walk hand in hand. Suffering and shame were his lot, experiences presumably indicating divine disfavor. He possessed no particular status or quality that would mark him as a representative and authoritative character. Thus, astonishment is recorded in v. 1, at the outset. All of this was incredible, unless divine power could make use of human weakness. Weakness it had used, summoning them to a general reassessment of social and religious values, a change veiled in obscurity. Revelation works in its own ways.

Together with this fresh evaluation of God's ways came a different perspective upon the servant's sufferings: They were in behalf of those speaking, who thereby acknowledge their sinful state, despite any temporal security they may have enjoyed (vv. 4-6). Verses 7-9 add to infirmities suggestions about legal judgment and violent suffering. Since illness and violence are the chief traditional modes of suffering, the experiences of the servant fit a general and comprehensive portrait, individual but catholic. This is a particular life and death sketched in terms broad enough to be typical. The poet eludes any efforts to pin down the servant's identity while rebuffing interpretations of his subject as a composite or corporate figure. The electric majesty and vibrant enigma of his creation reside in the tension between these two poles, these two thieves of meaning.

The structure of vv. 7-9 resembles that of the creed, for which it is a model. In these words of Deutero-Isaiah we may catch a glimpse of the materials utilized in the theological workshop of early Christianity, the laboratory of the Holy Spirit. Verses 10-11a speak of the postmortem vindication, yet elusively so, without speaking, for example, of resurrection. So concludes the people's story.

Surrounding the narrative is a frame. Isa. 52:13-15 and 53:11b-12 constitute God's announcement, the divine interpretation of what has transpired. The opening intentionally recalls 42:1-4. Both parts cohere; both frame and narrative relate both humiliation and exaltation. Humans have come to see things as God sees. This structure is an essential interpretive model for understanding the message of Christ's life, death, and resurrection. Meaning does not lie within the narrative, does not emerge from the plot, but from interpretation. The resurrection, not accessible to witnesses, is confessed by faith as God's interpretation of Christ. In their determination to prevent this interpretation from being a matter of "obvious fact," Mark and John focus upon the cross as the locus of revelation. This perspective informs and shapes the observance of Good Friday. The first reading states the theme of triumph proclaimed by God and acknowledged by mortals who had come to see that things are not as they seemed to be. We have become the narrators of Isaiah 53.

Episcopal Alternate: Genesis 22:1-18. This passage is discussed among the readings for the Easter Vigil.

Episcopal Alternate: Wisdom 2:1, 12-24. Occasional use of this alternate allows the probably larger congregations of Palm Sunday to hear the selection from Isaiah. Wisdom 2–5 is heavily indebted to the Servant Songs, the meaning of which its author struggles to understand in the face of adversity and the lack of vindication. The authors of Wisdom, Hebrews, and the Fourth Gospel share elements of a kindred religious environment and can often illuminate one another. This selection takes up, in diatribe style, the arguments of the wicked, the persecutors of God's servants and children. They set forth sensible commonplaces, casually embracing the doctrine of might makes right and the view that victims deserve blame for their state. They smart at the accusations of the righteous. The resultant irony is not unlike that of the Fourth Gospel. Verses 21-24 clarify the difference between appearance and reality. The wicked are blind to God's purposes, which are manifest in creation. Spiritual death is the fate of those who will not recognize God's intentions for the human race. Effective proclamation building upon this passage requires that the views of the wicked will not be treated as mere creatures of straw.

SECOND LESSON

Lutheran/Roman Catholic: Hebrews 4:14-16; 5:7-9. (A few introductory remarks on Hebrews will be found under the second lesson for Monday in Holy Week, above). The general theme is the movement of the wandering people of God toward ultimate rest. Hebrews 4:14—5:10 states themes later chapters will develop in elaboration. Hebrews alternates doctrinal and parenetic sections, keeping the relation between indicative and imperative in the forefront. Verses 14-16 are exhortations to maintain what is possessed and to press ahead. In verse 14 there is an identification of the common title "Son of God" with that of high priest. Jesus belongs to a different order of priesthood from those who must make their offerings again and again. The passage through the heavens does not here refer to negotiating hostile spheres of power, but to the goal of the journey: rest in the heavenly sanctuary. Behind this imagery is the widespread view of the cosmos as a heavenly temple.

Verse 15 juxtaposes to this affirmation of exaltation a clear statement of humiliation. This is not a deity without appreciation of human weakness. We may be likely to regard those who have fallen and recovered as more "sympathetic," but this is not the case here. The basis of Christ's sympathy is his experience of genuine temptation, from which he remained sinless. Sinlessness is evidently for the author a genuine human possibility. Both status and sympathy encourage believers to pray with full confidence in being heard. The imagery is cultic, but the context in view is probably not liturgical. The receipt of mercy cancels the past while grace provides strength for what is to come.

Verses 7-9 are, in the original, a single convoluted sentence of which the heart is v. 8. Verse 7 utilizes traditional images of piety and will gain little if seen as a summary of the Gethsemane episode. Through the elaborate prose and commonplaces shines a truly human figure, whose prayers were fervent yet reverent (cf. 4:16), and who was heard. Nonetheless, he suffered. "Education through suffering" (*pathei mathein*) was a shopworn proverb. The author seeks to revive it through the injection of new meaning. The full obedience that stems from real learning comes to light only with the often painful discovery of what God's will calls one to do. The "having been made perfect" of v. 9 refers to this identification with his mission. One will not do wrong to apply it to John 19:30 (which uses the same verb). Perfection is for redemption both its means and its result. Christ actually changed and was fashioned for the elevated position he now occupies. For the readers this provides both assurance of salvation and directions for the road ahead. We cannot be better off than Jesus.

Episcopal: Hebrews 10:1-25. This passage requires a skilled and sensitive lector and careful selection of a version. There are three sections: 1. Verses 1-10: the old as a shadow of new reality. 2. Verses 11-18: application of the previous by contrasting the former cultic worship to Christ's sacrifice, with appeal to Scripture. 3. Verses 19-25: exhortation similar to 4:14-16 which introduces the subsequent section.

The surprise of v. 1 is not that the law is, in an image derived ultimately from one of Plato's most popular analogies, a shadow, but the introduction of futurity. One expects Hebrews to prefer spatial images. By combining the two the writer relativizes each and thus transcends both. This author knows that theological language is metaphorical. For what the NRSV renders "true form" he uses the cautious *eikon* (image). In accordance with the common preference for unity to plurality, the need to repeat sacrifices places them in the realm of the many that are at best a shadow of the one. Verse 3 implies that in the new order sin can be forgotten, truly eradicated. The old prophetic critique of placid reliance upon cultic activities is here infused with the view that such actions belong to the fleshly, superficial sphere.

Verse 5 supports this with a provocatively ascribed quotation from Psalm 40, in which Christ is described as entering the world, rather than heaven. The entrance in question is not the moment of incarnation but the occasion of his self-offering. Christ "said" this because his act of salvation spoke in a way that gave the passage its meaning here. The psalm is thus an oracle to be interpreted in the light of the Christ-event (vv. 8-9). The climax of this argument appears in v. 10. The author states that Christ's sacrifice effected the sanctification ascribed to believers in the tradition. "Will" is crucial. The RSV interprets this as God's will, but v. 9 suggests that the volition of Christ is in mind. Animals are not sacrificed in accordance with their will. His will included the offering of his body. With "once for all" the writer returns to the "one versus many" theme of the opening and closes with an assertion of uniqueness.

Verses 11-18 are a summary with repetition of earlier principles and themes. Earthly priests stand at the altar day after day whereas Christ sits exalted in heaven, at rest. Verse 12 pulls together many of Hebrews' leading themes. It could stand as a summary of the book. In v. 13 there is a suggestion of more yet to come, the temporal dimension that the text is beginning to exploit. Verse 14 identifies the redeemed with the redeemer. This section also makes use of Scripture, the famous "new covenant" passage from Jeremiah, which the author pushes in such a way as to include the forgiveness of sins within the inscription of a new law in human hearts. This quotation stresses the results of the sacrifice of Christ.

The final section (vv. 19-25) is a single Greek sentence incorporating the "virtues" of faith, hope, and love into imperatives based upon the now established indicatives. The death of sacrifice has blazed a trail down a new road filled with fresh possibilities. Those do not excuse one from loving activity and participation in communal worship and life.

The polarities of time and space have become for the author of Hebrews tools to explain how a shameful death could be the decisive saving event. His emphasis upon Christ's will conforms to the view that categories like heavenly and eternal are media for projecting the essential human realities, which are inner and spiritual. The new covenant is written in our hearts, in blood.

GOSPEL: JOHN 18:1—19:42

The Passion according to John.   Readers may wish to consult also the parallel material for Passion/Palm Sunday. The Passion according to St. John has long enjoyed its privileged position as the Gospel text for this day. Every year reveals new opportunities and new insights. In outline this material is quite similar to Mark's, but there are important differences, including the absence of a trial before the Sanhedrin and a lengthy account of the Pilate trial, different chronology, various "omissions," and, most notably, the different characterization of Jesus. This Passion belongs to Good Friday because its hero is already victorious, sovereign, and superior to his adversities. Since the onset of his "hour" he has been glorified (13:1).

Behind these differences stand different forms of theological understanding and expression. If the Passion seems a bit anticlimactic in John, a narrative exposition of what 1:11 had long ago announced, "he came to what was his own and his own people did not accept him," this is because Jesus' entire mission has been one of judgment and trial (*krisis*). He repeatedly visits the city of his destiny, during which elements of the "trial" occur. Moreover, the trial of Jesus, from the Johannine perspective, continues to the present, reenacted wherever his message is proclaimed. The Passion narrative proper is the culmination of that message (cf. 18:19) and the narrative theological exposition of the elevation of the Son of Man. This theological understanding motivates the use and presentation of the material. This Passion has been shaped to enhance its dramatic qualities and may be divided into "acts" in which pairs of dominant characters oppose one another. Time and place are exploited for symbolic meaning.

I. 18:1-11—Arrest. The time is *night* (cf. 13:30). Peter and Jesus are set in contrasting roles. Nothing here resembles the agony of Gethsemane. When the authorities approach, Jesus takes the initiative in interrogation. They practically collapse at his "I am he" (*ego eimi*) and Jesus must, in effect, scoop them up and guide them on to the "police station." The forces arrayed for his arrest include almost all of the military and law enforcement personnel available, together with representatives of the leading parties. The appearance of this throng, complete with lamps and torches, seems unsuitable for the surreptitious capture of an accused subject. As a symbol of the powers of the world bringing futile "light" into a darkness of their own manufacture it suits very well.

Peter's brief venture into violent resistance reveals his misunderstanding of discipleship. Soon he will be overcome with cowardice issuing from the same source. Peter acts against the will of God and trusts human military glory rather than heavenly radiance (cf. 12:43). One who has not listened slices away the ear of a slave named "king," in mistaken service to a king who will die like a slave.

II. 18:12-27—Affirmation and Denial. This unit includes four scenes conducted in two "theaters." Jesus and Peter have a leading role in each locale.

A. Verses 12-14. The stage is set, together with a reminder of Caiaphas' intentions regarding Jesus and the attendant irony.

B. Verses 15-18. Peter enters the outer yard by denying Jesus. A mysteriously anonymous disciple is also present.

C. Verses 19-24. Jesus is sent on after examination and abuse. He stands firmly upon his public record and declines the opportunity for clarification. As 12:37-50 stipulate, what he had said, he had said. (For another "trial," see 10:22-39). Justice is not to be expected or sought in such precincts. Condemnation will come from all that he has done and said rather than from a particular deed. In the face of this refusal to refine or to recant the authorities become victims of their unrequited rage and resort to violence. Jesus emerges as the moral victor. The passage is a model for Christians under pressure from religious or political officials.

   D. Verses 25-27.   Peter affirms his denial. In contrast to his master, Peter does not speak plainly. The one who pulled out his sword in the garden now quavers before a portress. Physical weakness reflects spiritual malaise. Against Jesus' "I am he," he claims, "I am not he" (vv. 5 and 17). Both are in grave danger. Only one "escapes." The report is absolutely devastating in its quiet and simple pathos. This is a story about the conditions under which the creed is to be recited. Unlike Mark, there is no reference to despair. The cock crows, and we are left to invent appropriate reactions for Peter—or to admit that words will not suffice. Both Jesus and Peter have the last word in their respective theaters.

III. 18:28—19:16a—The Trial before Pilate.   A most penetrating irony permeates this dramatic confrontation. The irony relies upon the readers' superior knowledge, knowledge gained from the eyes of faith. Johannine irony is a literary expression of theological method. It functions on the basis of and in behalf of the conviction that signs are ambiguous, signs only to those who see that they point beyond rather than stand as things in themselves. As the structure of appearance begins to crack it becomes ever more incongruous. The appearance is the earthly; reality is heavenly. Those who find them congruent, if not identical, expose their lack of insight. The proponents of earthly religious and political "reality" are the leading priests and Pilate. Their object is preservation of the status quo. Each abandon their primary responsibility in pursuit of this goal.

   Middle-class Americans, at least, who see in this grounds for easy identification with Jesus may be continuing the tradition of self-deception. The majority of United States citizens usually agree with the Pilates and prelates when crime is on the rise and the established order under assault. Can one hear these verses without seeing in them a denunciation of the hypocritical calls to law and order that are willing to have a Barabbas released? The creed, "We have no king but Caesar," is the shibboleth of patriotic civil religion.

   There are seven scenes played on two stages. Understanding the structure of the trial is a prerequisite for perception of its meaning. It takes place in early morning (18:28). Darkness begins to wane as Jesus confronts the ruling power.

Text	Location	Characters	Action
A. 18:28-32	Outside	Pilate, leaders	Jesus handed over to Pilate
B. 33-38	Inside	Pilate, Jesus	First interrogation and result
C. 39-40	Outside	Pilate, leaders	Jesus or Barabbas?
D. 19:1-3	Inside	Soldiers, Jesus	Flogging, mockery
E. 4-7	Outside	Pilate, leaders then Jesus	Denial, display
F. 8-12	Inside	Pilate, Jesus	Second interrogation and result
G. 13-16	Outside	Pilate, Jesus, leaders	Condemnation

There is strict alternation between inside and outside. The scenes fall into two groups: 1. Scenes A–D, with the climax, "Here is the man," and the reply, "Crucify him!" 2. Scenes E–G, with the climax, "Here is your king," and the response, "Crucify him!" Each group focuses upon the identifications (simple person, king) and the subsequent acclamation ("crucify him!"). The beaten and humiliated one is, indeed, "King of the Jews." Through this slowly unfolding legal process those who would judge Jesus judge themselves. This is the Johannine view of judgment, and of the day of judgment.

A. The trial opens with wooden irony as those concerned for cultic purity pollute their souls. Both religious and civil laws will take a beating before this endeavor concludes. On judgment day creation reverts to chaos.

B. Pilate works with a view of kingship sufficient unto itself. Jesus' reply does not deny the political ramifications of the title, but states that his reign is an eschatological phenomenon, that the realm over which he rules stands over against the dominion of unbelief.

C. The discussion of Mark 15:6-15 (Sunday) treats the Barabbas episode in more detail. John presents a briefer account. The leaders would condemn the apparent criminal Jesus and release a real social enemy, one whose ideological offspring would later challenge Rome in a full-scale revolt.

D–E. Legally, whipping and abuse would come after judgment. Pilate perverts the law in order to find a compromise. As in Mark, the veneration of Jesus as a mock king piles irony upon irony. The sarcastic presentation of a pseudo-epiphany is a genuine manifestation of the divine. Only those who recognize in this object of ridicule an actual king may claim him as their heavenly lord. Verses 6-7 unveil the actual power of the hierarchy, who must beg the governor to execute justice as they would have it.

F. This scene raises suspense by retarding the action and allows Pilate's confusion and helplessness to surface. He has flitted back and forth from inside to outside like a flustered chicken. As are many who have no room for God in human affairs, he is inclined to be superstitious. Jesus declines to bandy with such degradation of the divine. Pilate then pulls rank, claiming to be a lord of Jesus' life and death. He is not. The reply does not divinize the Roman state—or others. It asserts that God's will is being carried out. The leading priests would quickly agree.

G. The crowd now takes a hand at reminding the governor of his responsibilities toward his lord and master. They do perceive that Jesus threatens Caesar but can only state this as a concrete and ironic absurdity. In this climactic scene all of the characters appear together on one stage. Verse 13 is ambiguous by intent. Although Pilate appears to be sitting upon his throne dispensing justice (he has, after all, been coerced), Jesus is the actual instrument of judgment, but not because he sentences. The rulers sentence themselves while the "judge" has only the apparatus of a legal bench, the appearance of power.

A wealth of circumstantial detail underscores the importance of the scene. The time is noon, at Passover. It is the hour for slaying paschal lambs. While the rulers and their minions plot legal murder on the Feast of Deliverance, God is working an act of deliverance. The verb rendered "away with him" (v. 15) can also mean "lift up." They will soon see their victim lifted up. Yet they will not "see." The manipulated masses bring their argument to its logical and frenzied conclusion: "We have no king but the emperor." With this affirmation of faith they judge themselves and abandon all pretense of believing in a sovereign God and bringer of eschatological peace. They elect earth over heaven, finding in the legal chaos they have created an ordered cosmos. Having achieved this "law and order," they take it for utopia.

Seated upon his throne, Pilate accepts their judgment. The wheels of execution begin to grind. For consolation he will have only the satisfaction of embarrassing the rulers through a seemingly petty revenge.

IV. 19:16b-42—Crucifixion, Death, and Burial. This account of Jesus' execution is rather restrained, colored throughout by a nearly visible aura of serenity. There is no suggestion of agony, no cry of dereliction. Jesus continues his ministry even upon the cross. Nor does this text include the apocalyptic images found in Mark: darkness, earthquake, indication of hours, and rending of the Temple veil. Likewise absent are mockery, crowd, and response from the other victims. The dominant themes are the inscription, the witnesses, the words, the piercing, and the elaborate burial. Layers of tradition clash. Even more prominent than in Mark are explicit citations from Scripture, which was searched by early believers to explicate the story and the meaning of Jesus. There are seven sections, ending with Jesus at rest in the tomb.

A. Verses 17-18: Passage to Golgotha and Crucifixion. Verse 17 resonates with 13. There are two places of judgment: Gabbatha and Golgotha. Jesus bears his own cross. A few words cover much ground.

B. Verses 19-22: The Inscription and a Debate. Such placards sought to enhance the deterrent effect of the punishment by showing which crime had not paid and who the victim was. This inscription is a short form of the creed, expressed in three languages to show its universality. Jesus sits upon his throne, drawing all people to himself. Pilate sees it as his retaliation upon the leaders and an ironic judgment of them. It *is* ironic, for by this piece of cheap revenge he joined his adversary, Caiaphas, in the role of unwitting prophet (11:47-53). Both see the action as expedient, albeit for different reasons.

C. Verses 23-25a: Division of the Spoils. If the inscription displays the universality of Jesus' salvation, the refusal to divide his garments apparently symbolizes the unity that should result from the community formed by his disciples.

D. Verses 25b-27: Message to the Witnesses. These appear early in John's Passion, with different names and roles. Prominent among them are the mother of Jesus and the so-called Beloved Disciple. Jesus unites them into a new family, the church, in which his form of presence will not be personal. As Good Shepherd he cares for his own even while laying down his life for them (cf. 10:11-18). The address to each echoes Pilate's words in presenting him to the crowd. The disciple took Jesus' mother "into his own" (lit.), for Jesus' own had not received him (1:11).

E. Verses (28-30)30b: Final Word and Death. The first part of this passage, which is probably a later addition, contains fulfillment of Scripture and, in particular, a link to Passover through the reference to hyssop (cf. Exod. 12:8). In the present text the last words seem to apply to that action. An earlier edition probably used "it is finished" to exemplify in vv. 25-27 the fulfillment of his ministry as bringing unity through self-giving love (cf. 13:1). Jesus does not collapse. He lays down his head, then his life. His death is the revelation of love.

F. Verses 31-37: Official Intervention Unwittingly Reveals Who Jesus Is. Verse 31 rudely thrusts us back from the majestic scene just completed into the world of religious propriety. While dispatching their victims the soldiers discover that Jesus has already expired. "None of his bones shall be broken" is not an otiose prooftext. Its source is the rubrics for preparing a paschal victim (Exod. 12:10). Thus, from another perspective, Jesus in dying has inaugurated liberation from the bondage of sin and death. Verses 34b-35 introduce a new subject. Verse 35 is very likely the addition of a later hand (cf. John 21), for the Fourth Gospel does not see human testimony as verification or true witness. There is dispute about v. 34b. Possibly secondary, it seems to portray a sign. Jesus' death (blood) is the source of living water. In the context of Christian theology, if not in the view of the Fourth Evangelist, the text refers to Jesus' death as efficating the sacraments. His ministry continues after his death through them.

The paschal lamb symbolism (probably pre-Johannine) and the allusion to blood should not lead to the conclusion that this Gospel presents Jesus' death as a sacrifice. The cross in John is first and foremost *revelation* of a most paradoxical nature. Jesus' death appears to be humiliation. In reality it is his exaltation. Preaching of the Johannine Passion that neglects this theological perspective will lack full fidelity to the text. The several authors of the NT present distinct theological perspectives that, canonization implies, deserve to be heard. John's perspective is that the cross is the glorious revelation of divine love.

H. Verses 38-42: Burial. The most desirable place for any sustained reflection upon the burial of Jesus is an early liturgy on Holy Saturday. John's account, which shows the continuing development of the burial legend, introduces the garden locale, rounding off the entire Passion, which began in a garden. Human life also began in a garden, as will the new life of Easter.

Joseph and Nicodemus provide enough supplies to embalm an emperor. How are we to understand their action and character? As examples of the power of Jesus' cross to draw all to himself? Or as the misplaced benevolence of wrong-thinking persons who had earlier lacked the courage of their convictions and only give public honor to a Jesus safely dead and out of the way? The Passion opened with one disciple pointing a finger and another pulling a sword. It closes with two semi-disciples giving Jesus honors shared by the rejected Servant (Isa. 53:9b). The Passion according to John leaves us wrestling with ambiguities, for revelation is never so clear and direct as we expect.

The Great Vigil of Easter

Lutheran	Roman Catholic	Episcopal	Common Lectionary
Gen. 1:1—2:3	Gen. 1:1—2:2	Gen. 1:1—2:2	Gen. 1:1—2:2
Gen. 22:1-18	Gen. 22:1-18	Gen. 22:1-18	Gen. 22:1-18
Exod. 14:10—15:1	Exod. 14:15—15:1	Exod.14:15—15:1	Exod. 14:15—15:1
Isa. 55:1-11	Isa. 55:1-11	Isa. 55:1-11	Isa. 55:1-11
1 Cor. 15:19-28	Rom. 6:3-11	Rom. 6:3-11	Rom. 6:3-11
Mark 16:1-8	Mark 16:1-7	Matt. 28:1-10	Mark 16:1-8

The Easter Vigil, of unusual length and at an inconvenient hour, is the most important liturgy of the year, the explanation and justification of Christian existence. There are four components: The Lighting of the New Fire, the Vigil proper, consisting of reading and response, Christian Initiation, and the first Eucharist of Easter. This is a liturgy of great drama filled with antitheses, including darkness and light, chaos and peace, slavery and freedom, sin and redemption, death and life. The service reenacts the passing over of God's people from the former member of each pair to the second. Although somber in tone, the Vigil opens with the celebration of Christ's light and is filled with joyful expectation and realization. This liturgy may begin at any time after sunset and before sunrise. The time of the resurrection is unknown. With morning comes its discovery.

The first four readings above represent a prudent selection from a maximum of twelve. The passage from Exodus must always be read. In the traditional setting each reading states a theme, followed by communal reflection in a psalm or canticle and closed with silence and a prayer applying the reading to the baptismal faith of Easter. The purpose of the readings is to tell in general the story of salvation. Those who preach on the Vigil readings might focus upon one or seek to pull together their grand sweep.

The Lutheran liturgy allows for the observance of a Vigil without a Eucharist, for which no particular proper readings are assigned. Lutheran preachers may choose the readings for Easter morning, treated in the succeeding volume of this series, or, presumably, select others. In any case the Gospel will be Mark 16:1-8, discussed below. Romans 6:3-11 is particularly appropriate for this occasion.

FIRST LESSON: GENESIS 1:1—2:2(3)

The Lutheran inclusion of 2:3 has the merit of speaking about the great Sabbath rest, the goal of the religious life. Within the Vigil this reading provides the context for salvation by stating God's intentions for the world and the human species, for whom God has particular designs. The story recounts the movement from chaos to rest, disorder to peace. In this material from the P source, the author subordinates all other issues to that of creation. Creation itself is an act of vocation, a summons into existence by authoritative word. Humanity is the only species which reflects some aspect of God. The bestowal of the image is the first biblical reference to God's risky self-offering. That this image is male and female does not mean that God is one, both, or neither, but that all humans possess it. The account ends with a benediction of rest. Throughout it the sense of order is communicated with the refrain-like phrase that completes the description of each day's activity. The creation story is not a scientific outline of how life came to be but an invitation to praise the source of all life and goodness.

SECOND LESSON: GENESIS 22:1-18

Sometimes love means breaking promises. The promise had been made and the deal done. Genesis 12:2 promised, in black and white, that from Abraham a great nation would come, a source of blessing for the whole earth. At more than long last a son arrived, the fulfillment of the promise. Then comes this story: God tells the patriarch to sacrifice Isaac.

What does Abraham, who had shrewdly pressed God against the wall for the sake of some Sodomites, do? He obeys in silence. The narrative recounts his homely preparations, the journey, his sensitive exclusion of the attendants, and their walk together. Once more he is addressed, this time by the child, with a question, to which he responds: "God will provide a lamb." The journey proceeds. In due course all is ready and the victim, bound to prevent resistance, is ready for the knife. Then Abraham is addressed for a third time, with a prohibition. Is there a lamb dropped from the sky? No, a kid caught in thorns. This is offered.

Then a fourth voice, reiterating the promise. Who has been tested? Abraham or God? Does God know the plot, or is v. 12 revelation to the Almighty, a change in the plans of God? In Holy Week the promises of God collide with God's tests. Faith means acceptance of both. "The Lord will provide a lamb" is not a blind affirmation that providence is a guarantee of bailouts. Abraham happened to glance about, and detected a *kid*. God writes straight with crooked lines. Isaac is the innocent initiate, Abraham the sage presider. To look at this as a game played by God to check out the extent of Abraham's reliability, Russian roulette with Isaac as expendable ammunition, does not do it full justice. Life may spring up surprisingly where death alone seems to loom, life trapped in gloomy thickets. Even with a *deus ex machina* this is a disturbing story. Love sometimes means keeping promises, including promises of obedience.

THIRD LESSON: EXODUS 14:10—15:1

This is *the* biblical story of deliverance, one that has sustained the children of Israel for millennia and provided Christians and others with a model for hope in the face of oppression and in the course of frightening journeys. The exodus is a source of symbols used again and again but not made trite. We read and hear this story in order to identify ourselves with it and it with our experiences. This narrative and its incidentals provide metaphors for Christian existence. With this process comes the danger of spiritualizing the text to the point that it no longer seems to speak of genuine physical deliverance from political oppression.

The context (esp. 14:5) discloses that, as in the Passion story, two plans are in effect: that of Pharaoh and that of God. By pursuing his own plan (or that of the Hebrews) Pharaoh unwittingly fulfills the plan of God. The exodus looked good until the Egyptian army appeared. The people's lament (vv. 11-12) closely parallels the Egyptian view expressed in 14:5. Even relationships of bondage terminate only with some pain. Neither Egyptian nor Hebrew contemplates the possibility that God may act. The people are thus told to keep still and come to know that God is God. The Egyptians will learn the same thing by not keeping still.

The blending of two sources leaves both supernatural (Moses' rod) and natural (wind) explanations of the sea's parting, leaving us to wonder whether either is adequate. The description of the antithetical experiences is graphic. Verse 30 gives a summary interpretation: The Hebrews had changed their earlier view and come to see that God could act. They did not choose to regard their escape as due to a fortunate shift of the wind. With trust in God came trust in God's servant, Moses (cf. Isa. 52:13—53:12).

We, too, have passed over in the gloom of night from the death of slavery to the life of freedom, from the death of sin represented in a pillar of cloudy ash to the life of grace illumined by the fiery pillar of the paschal candle; we, too, have passed through the grave of water to walk on dry land, sustained with bread from heaven. Now begins the rest of the journey to the promised land. It will be neither brief nor easy.

The lesson closes with the first verse of the triumphal song in the assumption that the people will sing 15:1-19 in affirmation of their participation in the events. The triumph is not military. God did the fighting. This is a victory of faith.

FOURTH LESSON: ISAIAH 55:1-11

The close of Deutero-Isaiah provides a fitting conclusion to the Servant Songs that form the core of readings from the Hebrew Bible during Holy Week. At another level it supplements the baptismal imagery discovered in the Exodus story with eucharistic symbols. Even more important than both of the preceding is the character of this passage as an invitation to partake of the utopian bounty of a God whose ways are not our ways. Holy Week has much to say about those strange ways. We are summoned to eat and drink, to find salvation *now,* but this invitation has been extended not only to us but to all whom God has made. The Creator celebrated in Genesis 1 is also ruler of history and has designs that far exceed anything we can ask for or imagine. These designs do not work like magic. They must first be heard.

EPISTLE: ROMANS 6:3-11

This reading looks back at the Vigil in that it makes specific Christian application of the exodus symbols of slavery and freedom, death and life. Its immediate context comes from the preceding baptisms/renewal of baptismal vows and the Easter proclamation. Two questions are addressed: What does it mean that I (and you) have been baptized? What is the meaning of Christ's resurrection to us?

Paul's answer reflects the basic Christian understanding of the unity of the death and resurrection. Paul interprets the resurrection of Christ in apocalyptic terms as the turning point of the ages, the decisive claim of eternity upon history. Baptism is how Christians appropriate this newness, through being possessed by the heavenly Lord. His focus is upon the present life of faith governed by hope for the future. We have participated in Christ's death and shall participate in his resurrection. The apostle takes care to state that resurrection is not a present possession. Verse 4 does not follow the logical parallel: "have died . . . have risen," but it does present the consequence of burial with Christ as the possibility of walking in the newness of life. The resurrection of Christ rules us. The result is freedom from sin and from the ultimate dominion of death. World, flesh, and devil live and even thrive, but they need not be arbitrators of our existence. "Alleluia! Christ our Passover has been sacrificed for us. Therefore let us keep the Feast. Alleluia!" Baptism is the link between these two references to "us." It makes keeping the feast a genuine possibility.

Because Paul had experienced in Corinth, at least, the effects of the claim to be living the resurrected life, he is quite circumspect. Verse 5a, with its difficult words smoothly rendered by the NRSV, focuses upon Jesus' death as the model for Christian life. In the context of solemn vows recently renewed, his nontriumphal stance is not something to gloss over. New life is the opportunity to live the kind of life of love for others that Jesus lived, including his death.

GOSPEL

The Episcopal lectionary alone retains Matt. 28:1-10 as the fixed Gospel for the Great Vigil. The others follow the annual rotation. After a general paragraph, both Mark and Matthew will be treated. Readers may benefit by a perusal of both, as the differences help reveal the message of each evangelist.

The New Testament contains many brief creedal statements that have inspired and shaped the Christian creeds. There are also creedal *stories*, such as that of the empty tomb. Both have the function of setting forth the indicative of salvation. Creedal stories intend to explicate the faith through narrative form and symbol. They should not be read as if they were creedal statements, for they include implicit imperatives and are potentially more subtle and ambiguous.

Lutheran/Roman Catholic/Common: Mark 16:1-8. The tendency of current scholarship is to assign responsibility for the shape of this pericope to the evangelist, regardless of sources. The text of Mark is so familiar to us that we can only with difficulty grasp the element of newness and surprise. The burial story leaves no suggestion that the funeral arrangements were lacking. Through this narrative dissonance the author signals a new and discontinuous beginning to the story. Are we to see the women's mission as approved? Not according to 14:3-9. What they come to do is redundant.

Chronological references burden v. 2. They conjure up crucial passages. "Very early" marked an important point in Jesus' opening ministry (1:35), played a role in a crucial parabolic saying (13:35), and denoted the moment of Jesus' delivery to Pilate (15:1). The women's question heightens dramatic suspense for initial readers and provides an ironic touch for those who know the story.

Epiphanic features color vv. 4-5, but they are not typical. We should expect an angel. There is instead, notably, a youth, dressed, notably, in white. The youth confronts them with a message, to which a casual reference to the tomb is appended. His message is equally unusual. The title is not "The Risen One" but still "The Crucified One." Priority is given to absence (cf. 13:21) rather than to resurrection. There is no encouragement to look for appearances. The plurality of allusions compel further contemplation. Who is this youth in white? Mark 14:51-52 featured a similar figure. White clothing is appropriate to an initiate, a martyr, and to a "candidate" for public office. How does one relate this scene to the Transfiguration (9:2-8) and the various sayings about the coming Son of Man? These are intriguing mysteries.

The techniques of vv. 5-6 use the apparatus of apocalyptic. The facts are a moved stone and an apparently empty tomb, neither miraculous. How is one to explain? The leading probabilities would be some kind of mischief, such as robbers or a piece of deceit engineered by persons bent upon perpetuating the movement. The young one functions like the interpreting angel of apocalypses (cf. Revelation) in that he gives the correct answer. The empty tomb is not cheap apologetic. It expresses in story form the origin of Easter faith in revelation that takes the form of interpretation. More compelling naturalistic explanations were available. Truth emerges through disclosure of what God has actually done. There is no description of the resurrection itself, for that is inaccessible, an event of eternity, not time. The revelation takes the form of a confession that Jesus is "not here," no longer within the temporal-spatial order. Christ has been translated into the next age or heaven. Mark 16 thus proclaims the resurrection as an apocalyptic event rather than as a phenomenon of history, such as the battle of Waterloo. To place the resurrection within this world and its history would be reductionism, and Mark will have none of it. The absence of Jesus rather than the whereabouts of his body is the chief subject.

The wellspring of faith on this night of the spring of souls is the proclamation within the community of Jesus' faithful followers. Its herald is not an authority like Peter, whose status would serve as a warrant for the tradition, nor is it a celestial emissary. The proclaimer is a mere youth decked out like one of the newly baptized. That neophyte continues to play his role when those baptized in Eastertide share the message and office.

Verse 7 presents a commission (cf. 14:28), which directs those who first forsook Jesus and then Peter (the last to abandon him) to Galilee, the polar opposite to Jerusalem in Mark and the symbolic locale of the good news. Jesus will go before them and they will see him. "Going before" is eschatological. The "Pioneer and Perfecter of our faith," to borrow from Hebrews, is in some sense always ahead of us, a figure beckoning from beyond to take up the cross and follow. "You will see" is ambiguous also. It may refer to some appearance not to be recounted, to the parousia itself, or, not at all impossibly, to having the eyes of faith opened (cf. 8:22-26; 10:46-52).

As we ponder these remarkable possibilities, the last verse crashes upon us with clanging dissonance. The women, too, flee, finally aligning themselves with their male colleagues, frozen in silent fear. How is one to assess this astonishing conclusion? A concrete approach might see here a critique of Peter and company. They never got the word and should not be trusted. (Peter's authority was the source of later conflict, as in the debate behind Galatians 1–2.) The traditional reading optimistically supplements the text: The story did eventually get out, somehow, and Peter and the others were transformed and even shared their master's fate. Those who admire irony would seek neither to gloss over 16:8 nor to see in it rejection of the original disciples, but to regard the unfinished conclusion as shifting the burden to the reader: we who hear this story are now responsible to share it. On Easter Even, at least, the last option recommends itself. Resurrection belief demands witness and mission. The ball is in our court, and we are challenged to defeat fear and shatter silence.

Nonetheless, the mystery of this ending will remain to haunt us. Both Matthew and Luke revised and expanded it, not to mention the editors who supplied the majority of Markan manuscripts with "improved" conclusions. This ending has not been popular. If the challenge to break the silence is a major paschal emphasis, there is another. In order to resolve the confusion of the ending one must go back to the beginning and read the Gospel once more, seeking clues that will help to unravel some of this mystery and dissonance. Mark 16:1-8 is both a new beginning and a summons to "The beginning of the good news of Jesus Christ, the Son of God" (1:1). Like the close of *Finnegan's Wake*, the end of Mark leads into the beginning. "The end," wrote T. S. Eliot, "is where we start from." On most paschal candles there is inscribed an Alpha and an Omega.

Episcopal: Matthew 28:1-10. Comparison reveals that Matthew has rounded off and transformed Mark's account of the visit to the tomb and its aftermath, eliminating much of the ambiguity but not altering the fundamental message. Two Marys (Matthew is fond of pairs) arrive as soon as is feasible to view the tomb, continuing the ministry of witness described in 27:55. They have no plans to anoint the body and thus no concerns for the stone. Examination of the immediately preceding and following pericopes will illustrate Matthew's contrast between the behavior and character of the leading human characters: a group of (presumably) hardened soldiers and two supposedly timid and inconsequential women.

At the tomb there is a typical epiphany, with earthquake (cf. 27:51), and an angel who removes the stone and sits majestically upon it and looks in every way as an angel should. Epiphanies overwhelm; in the face of this one the soldiers collapse (like the disciples in Gethsemane). Only the women endure the announcement, which includes the usual exhortation to courage, a reminder that Jesus had prophesied his rising, and a clarification of Mark 16:7 that makes the reference to "going ahead" definitely geographic. They are to examine the tomb but briefly, for their mission requires haste. With haste they obey, moved by a curious combination of fear and great joy. One could see this as supplementing Mark, but there is to Easter an awesome fear that does not diminish joy nor is cancelled by it.

The women are met (cf. 25:1-13) by the risen one (whose appearance and nature Matthew does not describe, leaving blanks we are not to fill in), who greets them joyously. They worship without restraint (cf. 28:17) in the form proper before a great king. Christ repeats the angelic message with specific directions that the disciples are to go to Galilee, raising tension and preparing the way for vv. 16-20.

Some may find this a bit of a disappointment in comparison with Mark. The First Evangelist prefers to narrate apocalyptic *stories* rather than exploit apocalyptic *symbols* (e.g., 27:51-53). If these are viewed as parabolic, the result is less unlike Mark than would first appear. Matthew depicts the full grandeur of an epiphany as a symbol of Easter. Such events are dangerous if not given interpretation. The women could withstand the threat because they were prepared to listen. The tomb proves nothing. As in Mark, proclamation alone is effective. If an angel is the original source and Jesus confirms the angel's message, the women became the bearers of tradition. Had the disciples refused to trust them (note the contrast in vv. 11-15), the story would have come to an end. Their vision of the risen Savior was both a "reward" and a symbol of their courage to endure the awesome display of raw divinity and their willingness to hear and respond.

There is little joy in Matthew's Gospel, but this Easter story is filled with it. If Mark leaves the decision in the reader's hands, Matthew provides in the women models of what Easter joy means: the compulsion to rush out and share the message, in which act the Risen One becomes manifest. This mission and this encounter we can likewise share. Anyone can repeat the angelic announcement "Christ is risen." Easter bursts forth when others react. "Indeed!"